40 DAYS TO
TOTAL
FORGIVENESS

R.T. KENDALL

CHARISMA
HOUSE

40 DAYS TO TOTAL FORGIVENESS by R. T. Kendall
Published by Charisma House
Charisma Media/Charisma House Book Group
600 Rinehart Road, Lake Mary, Florida 32746

Visit the author's website at www.rtkendallministries.com.

Library of Congress Cataloging-in-Publication Data

Names: Kendall, R. T., 1935- author.
Title: 40 days to total forgiveness / by R.T. Kendall.
Description: Lake Mary, Florida : Charisma House, [2019] | Includes
  bibliographical references and index.
Identifiers: LCCN 2019007063 (print) | LCCN 2019012870 (ebook) | ISBN
  9781629996325 (e-book) | ISBN 9781629996318 (trade paper : alk. paper) |
  ISBN 9781629996325 (ebk.)
Subjects: LCSH: Forgiveness--Religious aspects--Christianity. | Forgiveness
  of sin.
Classification: LCC BV4647.F55 (ebook) | LCC BV4647.F55 K44 2019 (print) |
  DDC 234/.5--dc23
LC record available at https://lccn.loc.gov/2019007063

19 20 21 22 23 — 987654321
Printed in the United States of America

To

Jonathan, Ghazala, and Ann

CONTENTS

SECTION III:
WHOM DO YOU NEED TO FORGIVE?

SECTION IV:
DO YOU KNOW IF YOU'VE FORGIVEN—TOTALLY?

SECTION V:
ARE YOU READY TO BE SET FREE FROM THE PAST?

Preface

SOME READERS MAY recall my book *40 Days With the Holy Spirit*. This was a follow-up to my book *Holy Fire*. We decided to apply this concept to my book *Total Forgiveness*. What you have in this book is an outline of my previous book by this title. You may read one chapter a day devotionally alongside your own time of prayer and Bible reading—but never as a substitute for such!

I am indebted to my editor, Debbie Marrie, for doing a lot of hard work in transferring the basic concepts of *Total Forgiveness* to this smaller volume. I must say, however, that the reader should remember that my original book, *Total Forgiveness*, is still in print and includes details not found in this book.

This book is dedicated to three special friends in London: Jonathan and Ghazala David and Ann Lloyd-Jones. These three friends have provided wonderful fellowship for Louise and me when we have been in London.

—R. T. KENDALL

What Is Total Forgiveness?

Father, forgive them.
—LUKE 23:34

WE ALL HAVE a story to tell. As you begin to read this book, you may think it is impossible to forgive your unfaithful husband or wife. You may feel you cannot forgive your abusive parent. You may feel you cannot forgive someone for what was done to your son or daughter. How can we forgive the church leader who took advantage of his position? What about the person who lied to us or about us, or the person who believed those lies? The list of potential offenses is endless. There are rapists out there. Child abusers. Murderers. Often closer to home there are unkind or unloving relatives and former close friends who have become enemies.

Years ago I wrote a book called *Total Forgiveness,* and it quickly became my best-selling book. This convinced me that it is a much-needed message for our time. Since writing it, I have received many letters and emails from people. One particularly heartrending letter came from a couple who told me what their son-in-law had done to their daughter and grandchildren. It was an awful story. "Are you saying we must totally forgive our son-in-law?" they asked. That was a hard question to answer. But I had to tell them the truth: yes, they must learn to forgive. My heart went out to them. I can only imagine the pain they had experienced. But total forgiveness is the only way they will ever find freedom and release from the offense.

I have received many other letters that describe everything from infidelity to incest to rape to lying and slander. It is enough to make me consider very carefully indeed what I preach and write in my books. People experience real pain when they or someone they love is hurt by another person. It is often harder to forgive when the one who has been hurt is someone you love deeply, especially your child. I find it much easier to forgive what people have said or done to me personally than what they have said or done to my children.

It is not unlike Corrie ten Boom's having to forgive the prison guard who was so cruel to her sister Betsie. Corrie saw this man viciously abuse her sister—who died shortly afterward—when the sisters were in prison for protecting Jews in Holland during World War II. Years later Corrie was seated on the platform of a church, preparing to speak in a service, when she spotted this very man in the audience. She struggled in her heart. She prayed in desperation for God to fill her heart with the love of Jesus. He did, but forgiveness became even more of a challenge when after the service this guard rather glibly said, in so many words, how good God is to forgive all of us. She wondered how sorry he was.[1]

It is often easier, then, it seems to me, to forgive what is done to us personally than to forgive what is done to those we love. But it is still very hard to forgive those who have hurt us directly, especially when they do not feel the slightest twinge of conscience. If our offender would put on sackcloth and ashes as a show of repentance, it would be much easier to forgive him or her.

But remember, at the foot of Jesus' cross no one seemed very sorry. There was no justice at His "trial"—if you could even call it that. A perverse glee filled the faces of the people who demanded His death: "'Crucify him!' they shouted" (Mark 15:13). Furthermore, "those who passed by hurled insults at him, shaking their heads and saying, 'So! You who are going to destroy the temple and build it in three days, come down from the cross and save yourself!'" (Mark 15:29–30). They shouted, "Let the Christ, this King of Israel, come down now from the cross, that we may see and believe" (Mark 15:32, ESV).

What was Jesus' response? "Father, forgive them, for they do not know what they are doing" (Luke 23:34). This must be our response as well.

Jesus could have said, "I forgive you." But such words might have been misinterpreted and wasted, like casting His pearls before swine. (See Matthew 7:6.) Instead Jesus asked the *Father* to forgive them, a far grander gesture. Asking the Father to forgive them showed that not only had He forgiven them and released them from their guilt but also He had asked His Father not to punish or take revenge on them. It was not a perfunctory prayer; Jesus meant it. And it was gloriously answered! These offenders were among the very ones Peter addressed on the day of Pentecost and who were converted. (See Acts 2:14–41.)

When I wrote *Total Forgiveness*, my goal was to encourage anyone who has had a problem with forgiving those who have hurt him or her, however deeply. I now write this companion book, *40 Days to Total Forgiveness*, to help you focus on the steps to such forgiveness. Many people who read this book will have been through far worse than what I have experienced. But I have come to believe that the only way to move beyond the hurt and go forward in life is through total forgiveness. My prayer is that this simple forty-day book will change your life through the power of forgiveness just as my own was changed.

Many have studied forgiveness over the years. One researcher has identified three degrees, or levels, of forgiveness:[2]

1. Detached forgiveness—where there is a reduction in negative feelings toward the offender, but no reconciliation takes place.

2. Limited forgiveness—where there is a reduction in negative feelings toward the offender and the relationship is partially restored, though there is a decrease in the emotional intensity of the relationship.

3. Full forgiveness—where there is a total cessation of negative feelings toward the offender and the relationship is fully restored.

This forty-day forgiveness journey goes deeper than those three levels. That's why I decided to use the phrase *total forgiveness* as the title of my first book on this topic—and all the books related to it, including this one. The forgiveness you're discovering is not detached or limited or even full forgiveness; it is a type of forgiveness that must happen deeply and completely in the heart, and when it does, peace emerges and the Holy Spirit is able to dwell in you ungrieved, able to be utterly Himself.

Are you ready to experience this type of forgiveness? The choice is yours. I cannot promise you the journey ahead will be an easy one, but I can promise it will be worth it.

Clearing Up the Misconceptions

Forgiveness Is *Not* Approving or Justifying What Happened

As you begin day one, I want you to know I understand that forgiveness is no small task. It can be one of the hardest things you will ever have to do, especially if the hurt is severe. As I acknowledged in the introduction of this book, I know many of you reading this are dealing with things far more painful than anything I've ever had to endure. But I also believe that no matter how dark and devastating the experiences of your past have been, choosing total forgiveness is the pathway out of your pain.

I don't believe you've made this choice lightly; you might already sense the road ahead will be difficult and possibly painful. This book was designed to help you take daily steps toward the freedom awaiting you when you finally let go of the past. We'll begin by setting the record straight about some common misconceptions people have, starting with that by forgiving someone, you are approving or justifying what they've done.

Just as God forgives people without approving of their sin, we also must learn that forgiving people does not imply an endorsement of their evil deeds. We can forgive what we don't approve of because that is the way God has dealt with each of us.

God hates sin. In the Garden of Eden, He became angry with our first parents, Adam and Eve, because of their sin, but He still made garments of skin for them and clothed them (Gen. 3:21). This act of mercy demonstrated His forgiveness, even at that time. The garments of skin signified the sacrifice of blood that would be shed by the Redeemer who was to come.

In the New Testament, Jesus forgave the woman found in adultery, but He did not approve of what she did. He told her, "Leave your life of sin" (John 8:11).

So God did not approve of sin in biblical times—nor does He approve of sin today. We are to maintain a healthy respect and fear of God's justice and forgiveness: "But with you there is forgiveness, that you may be feared" (Ps. 130:4, ESV).

To *justify* means to make right or just. The *Oxford English Dictionary* says it means to "show [a person or statement or act, etc.] to be right or reasonable."[1] There is no way that evil can be justified. God will never call something that is evil "right," and He does not require us to do so.

In Moses' prayer for the Israelite people he did not offer a hint of justification for their behavior. Instead, he pointed out to God that the Egyptians would not think very highly of God's power or name if they saw Him obliterate His own people. While we are required to forgive, we should never attempt to make what is wrong look as though it is right.

PERSONAL REFLECTION

Have you ever been in a situation where you "forgave" someone in a way that condoned the person's behavior? How did the person respond? What would true forgiveness have done?

_____

_____

_____

_____

_____

Have you heard people try to justify their actions even after they received forgiveness? Have you ever caught yourself doing this? Pause and ask God to show you what you can do to avoid this trap as you continue your journey to total forgiveness.

_____

_____

_____

_____

DAY 2

Forgiveness Is *Not* Excusing or Pardoning What Happened

ANOTHER COMMON MISCONCEPTION is that forgiveness is excusing or pardoning what happened. We do not cover for the sins of other people. We do not point to circumstances in an attempt to explain away their behavior. While it is true that "every person is worth understanding," as Dr. Clyde Narramore says,[1] this does not include excusing their inappropriate behavior.

As Moses led the children of Israel across the desert toward the Promised Land, he was continually aggravated by their complaining. Eventually, after he had cried out to the Lord about the problem, he was offered a "new deal." God essentially said to him, "You have a sorry lot of people to lead, and they aren't following you very well. They have been stubborn and unteachable. I have decided to wipe them off the face of the earth and start all over again with a new nation." (See Numbers 14:11–12.) Moses rejected God's offer and interceded for the people. In his prayer he did not excuse their behavior; instead, he appealed to God's mercy: "In accordance with your great love, forgive the sin of these people, just as you have pardoned them from the time they left Egypt until now" (Num. 14:19). And God forgave them.

A pardon is a legal transaction that releases an offender from the consequences of his or her action, such as a penalty or a sentence. This is why we do not ask that the guilty rapist be exempt from punishment. He needs to pay his debt to society, and society must be protected from him.

I know of a lady who was raped by a person from a Middle Eastern country. At the time of the rape, she did not know he was from overseas; she found this out after he was caught. In the meantime she became a Christian. The police wanted her to testify at his trial. She was told he could be sent back to his homeland, which would mean he could be executed (the legal penalty for rape in his country).

She turned to me for advice. I counseled her to testify against this man. She had already forgiven him, but though she did not want to get him into trouble, if she did not testify, he would likely do it again. By the time she took the witness stand, there was no bitterness left in her heart; she was able to merely describe what had happened. As a result the man was sent back to his own country. We never heard what happened to the man after he was extradited, but the potential punishment that he faced did not have any bearing on the forgiveness that had been offered by his victim.

PERSONAL REFLECTION

Have you ever blamed your circumstances instead of asking for forgiveness? How much weight should you give circumstances when deciding if a person has done wrong?

_____

_____

_____

_____

_____

_____

Have you ever been in a situation—perhaps a court case or a simple matter of disciplining a child—where you had the power to forgive and to pardon? What did you do? Think about your decisions in such instances and why you made them.

_____

_____

_____

_____

_____

_____

DAY 3

Forgiveness Is *Not* Reconciling, Forgetting, or Pretending You're Not Hurt

FORGIVENESS AND RECONCILIATION are not always the same. Reconciliation requires the participation of two people. The person you forgive may not want to see or talk to you. Or he or she may have passed away since the time of the offense. Moreover, you may not want to maintain a close relationship with the person you forgive.

Reconciliation implies a restoration of friendship after a quarrel. When a husband and wife totally forgive each other, it will usually mean a reconciliation—but not always. The bitterness and the desire to punish the other person may be gone, but the wish to restore things to the way they were may not necessarily be so strong. If your spouse is unfaithful and sleeps with your best friend, both your marriage and your friendship will probably never be the same, no matter how genuine the forgiveness that is offered.

An injured person can forgive an offender without reconciliation. It is wonderful indeed if the relationship can be restored, but this must not be pressed in most cases. Some things can never be the same again. It takes two to reconcile, and there must be a total willingness on both sides.

Second Corinthians 5:19 tells us that God was in Christ, reconciling the world to Himself. But we still implore people on Christ's behalf: "Be reconciled to God" (v. 20). Why must we do this? Reconciliation doesn't really take place until both parties agree.

When people say we must "forgive and forget," I understand what is meant. They are equating true forgiveness with wiping the memory of the event from their minds. But literally to forget may not be realistic. It is usually impossible to forget meaningful events in our lives, whether positive or negative. Sometimes deep trauma may cause amnesia of the event, but that is not a healthy form of forgetfulness. Often the way back to sanity after experiencing this type of amnesia is to try to remember everything—in detail.

Love doesn't erase our memories. It is actually a demonstration of greater grace when we are fully aware of what occurred—and we still choose to forgive. God doesn't literally forget our sins. He *chooses* to overlook them. He knows full well what we have done—every sordid detail. But He chooses not to remember so as to not hold our sins against us. (See Hebrews 8:12.) That is precisely what we are to do; although we may not be able to forget, we can still choose not to remember.

Deep hurts may never be eradicated as though they never happened. The truth is, they did happen. But even if we cannot totally forget, we must not dwell on them.

It is ridiculous to think that we should have to keep a stiff upper lip when we have been injured by a spouse's infidelity or betrayed or molested or unjustly criticized.

God let David know how grieved He was over the king's sins of adultery and murder. God did not pretend not to be hurt. David was a man after God's own heart (1 Sam. 13:14), and yet God was ruthlessly impartial with David. He was very grieved indeed.

Jesus was obviously hurt when He was struck in the face by a high priest's official. He even asked the man, "Why did you strike me?" (John 18:23). After all, Jesus endured the cross and scorned, rather than denied, the shame (Heb. 12:2). And He was able to say, "Father, forgive them, for they do not know what they are doing" (Luke 23:34).

PERSONAL REFLECTION

Is there anyone in your life with whom you want to be reconciled but can't? Have you ever been genuinely reconciled with someone after an offense?

_____

_____

_____

_____

_____

_____

_____

How do you "forget" offenses?

_____

_____

_____

_____

_____

_____

Have you tried to pass off an offense as unimportant? Why did you downplay the depth of the hurt you experienced? Pause and ask God to help you avoid these traps on your journey to total forgiveness.

_____

_____

_____

_____

_____

_____

Forgiveness Is *Not* Denying What Happened or Not Taking It Seriously

DENYING THAT AN offense took place, or repression (suppressing what we really feel inside), is almost always unconscious. Some people, for various reasons, live in denial; that is, they refuse to admit or come to terms with the reality of a bad situation. It is sometimes painful to face the facts, and at times denial seems to be an easy way out.

Repression almost always has negative consequences for our psychological well-being. We often do it involuntarily because in some situations the pain is too great to deal with on a conscious level. But repression cannot remove the wound. Even when the pain is pushed down into the cellar of our subconscious mind, it will still come out one way or another, often causing high blood pressure, nervousness, irritability, or even a heart attack.

Many victims of child abuse repress the memory of the event. The conscious mind cannot accept that a parent, a trusted friend, or a relative would do such a thing, so the victim often lives in denial. Rape victims experience the same phenomenon.

Total forgiveness is not carried out by repressing the offensive event. True forgiveness can only be offered after we have come to terms with reality—when we can admit, "This person actually did or said this to me."

We cannot truly forgive until we see clearly the offense we are forgiving and understand its seriousness.

Some people may think that in order to forgive, they must dismiss a wrong or pass it off as inconsequential or insignificant. But that is only avoiding the problem, possibly trying to make forgiveness easier. The greater victory for the one who does the forgiving is to face up to the seriousness—even the wickedness—of what happened and still forgive.

This is what God does. There is no sin too great for God to forgive. But He knows exactly what it is we've done and what it is He is forgiving. He doesn't say, "Come now, My dear, that's not too bad. I can easily wash *this* sin away." No. He sent His Son to die for sin, and Christ's sacrificial death proves just how serious a problem sin is. God doesn't pass our sins off as inconsequential, yet He forgives.

Total forgiveness is not being oblivious to what an offender did; it is not covering up, excusing, or refusing to acknowledge what happened. That would be living in denial. Some people choose to live in denial as a way of dealing with pain; this often happens during the time of grief when a loved one dies. But sooner or later the grieving person must come to terms with reality. As I said before, repression is almost never a good thing.

PERSONAL REFLECTION

Think about a situation in which someone you know denied he was hurt when it was obvious he had been. What was the short-term result? Did denial help or hinder forgiveness? What were the long-term effects?

_____

_____

_____

_____

_____

_____

_____

Pause and ask God to help you learn to recognize the seriousness of an offense while still offering grace.

_____

_____

_____

_____

_____

_____

_____

Forgiveness Is *Not* Blindness
to What Happened

SOME PEOPLE, ESPECIALLY those with an "overly scrupulous conscience," as some Puritans may call it, feel that to forgive is to be willfully and consciously blind to the sin that was committed. They feel that if they offer forgiveness, they are turning a blind eye to, or ignoring, the offense, and they believe that this would in effect be excusing a sin against God.

Willful blindness is slightly different from denial and repression, which we covered yesterday. Blindness is a conscious choice to pretend that a sin did not take place; denial and repression are usually unconscious and involuntary. Both are wrong and can be psychologically damaging.

When we play such word games with ourselves, we can delay coming to terms with our own responsibility to forgive. Someone who is trying to forgive an offense but is actually pretending that the event never happened will eventually explode and become an offender himself—all because he was not being true to the pain the original offense had caused.

Paul said that love "keeps no record of wrongs" (1 Cor. 13:5). But he did not mean that you must be blind to those wrongs. True forgiveness of a wrong does not pretend that no wrong is there. The Greek word used in this verse is *logizomai*, which means to reckon or impute. Paul essentially is saying that "love does not store a wrong"; that is, the wrong that was committed against us doesn't go into our "mental computer" to be reckoned with later. But the fact that there *is* something wrong, especially if it is staring you in the face, is not to be denied. In fact the Greek word translated "wrong" in this verse is *kakos*, which means "evil."[1] Because it is evil, it must be acknowledged. We cannot be blind to it. We should not pretend it didn't happen. That is not what total forgiveness means.

Sometimes if the person who hurt or wounded us is an authority figure or perhaps known to be very "godly," we may say to ourselves: "I didn't see this. I didn't hear this. This could not have happened; therefore, it didn't." But the truth is sometimes the people we admire the most can do the most hurtful things to us. And it is of no value to pretend we didn't see it happen.

It is no spiritual victory to think we are forgiving people when we are only avoiding facing up to their wrong behavior. It is, if anything, evading true forgiveness. It is as though we are saying to ourselves, "I want to forgive them, but I don't think I really could if they actually did what it seems they did." So we postpone recognizing the true offense in order to keep from experiencing the pain, and we let them carry on as though nothing happened.

Total forgiveness is achieved only when we acknowledge what was done without any covering up—and still refuse to make the offender pay for his or her crime. Total forgiveness is painful. It hurts when we kiss revenge goodbye. It hurts to think that the person is getting away with what he or she did and nobody else will ever find out. But when we know fully what the person did and accept in our hearts that he or she will be blessed without any consequences for the wrong, we begin to be a little more like Jesus, to change into the image of Christ.

PERSONAL REFLECTION

Think about a time when someone you respected—perhaps a friend, boss, or minister—committed a wrong that was too big or too painful to acknowledge. Did you find yourself denying that it could be true, even for a moment? How did you come to grips with it in the end?

_____

_____

_____

_____

_____

_____

_____

_____

_____

SECTION II

Can You Learn to Forgive?

Consider the Consequences

As we begin a new section focused on the question "Can you learn to forgive?" I feel it's important to paint a clear picture of what happens when you choose to forgive and, more importantly, what happens when you don't.

1. Consider the consequences if you do forgive.

In my own powerful experience with forgiveness that became the basis for my book *Total Forgiveness*, I explain that a good friend advising me to forgive told me, "Release them, and you will be released." I didn't think I could do it at the time, but my friend was right. The bondage wasn't worth holding on to my unforgiveness. The absence of seeing Jesus' face wasn't worth it. The lack of peace wasn't worth it. But getting that peace back (I had forgotten what it was like) was worth it all.

That inner peace and clear thinking are the consequences of choosing to forgive. They are closer than your fingertips, closer than the air you breathe. They are near you, even in your heart, but you are unable to experience them because of the resentment you are holding toward other people. Forgive them. Release them. Do it in your heart.

Refuse to dwell on plans for revenge or rehash painful

memories that rob you of time and sleep. Think only pleasant thoughts (Phil. 4:8). Who knows how God will use you down the road if—once and for all—you set your enemies free and never look back.

2. Consider the consequences if you don't forgive.

Jesus put this very strongly indeed: "If you do not forgive others their sins, your Father will not forgive your sins" (Matt. 6:15). That doesn't mean you won't be guided or looked after. God still guided and looked after me. But now I realize why I lost so much that I had once had. Great though God's plans for me may have been, He didn't bend the rules for me. He allowed me to get deep into debt and suffer the humiliation of having to be out of the full-time preaching ministry; I peddled vacuum cleaners as a door-to-door salesman for years, living under a cloud whereby nobody believed in me.

Whether I hurt my health in all this, I can't say. But in some people the refusal to forgive leads to countless physical ailments. Lack of forgiveness is aging; it puts lines on faces before they should come. In some cases it means sleeplessness.

My lack of forgiveness made it easy and natural to be bitter. I felt no conviction that it was wrong. Neither did God manifest Himself in any great power. I forfeited anointing that could have been mine though. The consequences of an unforgiving spirit add up to one thing: the bitterness isn't worth it.

The devil does not want you to forgive others; he loves it when you are bitter. This way he has access to you. He therefore will put up what appear to be good reasons for wanting your adversary to be punished—and by you, if at all possible. Those thoughts of revenge or imaginary conversations where you put that person in his or her place are inspired by him, by the way. He wants to rob you of time, energy, and joy. You can expect obstacles to be put in your way if you try to forgive. He will give you every opportunity and reason not to forgive, but the consequences of this are disastrous.

I believe there are five consequences for choosing to withhold forgiveness.

1. *The Holy Spirit is grieved.*

"And do not grieve the Holy Spirit of God, with whom you were sealed for the day of redemption" (Eph. 4:30). Your relationship with the Holy Spirit should be one of the most important priorities in your life. When the Holy Spirit is grieved, it causes a distortion in your thinking. The ungrieved Spirit is what enables you to cope. You want to be at your best, whether on the job, raising your children, or doing the work of the ministry. You do not want the Holy Spirit to be upset with you. Let's not forget that immediately after Paul admonished us not to grieve the Spirit, he added:

> Get rid of all bitterness, rage and anger, brawling and slander, along with every form of malice. Be kind and compassionate to one another, forgiving each other, just as in Christ God forgave you.
> —Ephesians 4:31–32

2. *You are left to yourself.*

A refusal to forgive means that God stands back and lets you cope with your problems in your own strength. Not many people want to live that kind of life—coping on their own without God's help. When one is left to oneself, unthinkable capabilities toward sin are given free reign. Not only that, but Satan is also able to get in. He will take advantage of you if he can. (See 2 Corinthians 2:11.) He will exploit that unforgiving spirit, play on your self-pity, and worst of all cause you to believe God is with you—that you are perfectly justified in your anger. Once that has happened, do not be surprised if at the end of the day you fall into other sins. You may even begin to do things that you never thought you would do. Once the devil gains entrance, you begin to compromise all sorts of things relating to money, sex, and integrity.

3. You force God to become your enemy.

> What causes fights and quarrels among you? Don't they come from your desires that battle within you? You desire but do not have, so you kill. You covet but you cannot get what you want, so you quarrel and fight. You do not have because you do not ask God. When you ask, you do not receive, because you ask with wrong motives, that you may spend what you get on your pleasures.
>
> You adulterous people, don't you know that friendship with the world means enmity against God? Therefore, anyone who chooses to be a friend of the world becomes an enemy of God.
>
> —JAMES 4:1–4

The reason God treats you like an enemy is because by not forgiving others, you are really saying, "God, move over; I want to do Your job"! You proclaim yourself judge, jury, and executioner, and you presume to take God's place. He alone is the righteous judge. Being righteous, He will do right. He will clear your name. He will deal fairly with those who hurt you. He feels what you feel. But if you decide to do His work for Him, He becomes your enemy. When you judge another, you never get away with it. Do not judge, and you won't be judged. Judge, and you will be judged. It's as simple as that.

4. You lose the potential of your anointing.

When you will not forgive, the anointing God may have given to you is lifted, and you will become like an empty shell. You may be able to continue for a while because the gifts of God are irrevocable (Rom. 11:29). You may flourish for a while; the momentum of other gifts may make you think you still have the anointing you enjoyed yesterday. But mark this down: bearing a grudge and trying to punish and get even will cut off your anointing. The loss will become apparent sooner or later—unless you choose to forgive, and forgive totally.

5. You lose authentic fellowship with the Father.

When it comes to forgiveness of sins, there are two levels. One is what you would call forensic; it refers to what is legal and is the essence of being justified. God legally declares that you are righteous. It is the way God sees you in Christ—legally, as if you had never sinned. But there is also the spiritual level, wherein not only are you declared righteous, but you also enjoy a spiritual experience that comes from being forgiven. You lose this experience when you are in a state of unforgiveness.

PERSONAL REFLECTION

Do you sense the Holy Spirit is grieved with you for any reason? Have you become an enemy of God? Are you at risk of losing the potential of your anointing or your heavenly reward? Take a moment to meditate on the Lord with an open heart toward making things right. Ask for forgiveness if you need to.

_____

_____

_____

_____

_____

_____

Imagine you have lived your whole life and someone is reading your biography. In one version of your life story your highest dreams were blocked by unforgiveness, and in the other you freely forgave and let God's highest purpose for you come to pass. How are the two versions different?

_____

_____

_____

_____

_____

_____

_____

_____

Resist Resentment and Revenge

As we begin day seven of this journey, we'll explore the manifestations of unforgiveness in someone's life. Examine your own life as you read, and see if you identify any of these attitudes and behaviors that surface when unforgiveness lurks in the heart.

Having an unforgiving spirit usually begins with resentment. Resentment develops when you hold a grudge and become inwardly bitter. You become preoccupied with hate and self-pity. You can't come to terms with the possibility that the person who committed such an awful act against you will not be caught. You want the person exposed; you want the person to be held up for the whole world to see what he or she has done.

Resentment leads to going over and over again in your mind what the offender did, recounting and reliving exactly what happened. You should not dwell on the incident or even think about it. It will not bring you any relief or release; instead, it will cause you to become even more churned up.

All this leads to wanting to get even, to take revenge. You become determined to make your offenders pay. And just how do you make your enemies pay for their crimes against you? One way is by threatening to tell what you know about them and keeping them paralyzed with fear. Perhaps you know a dirty secret about someone who offended you, and if you spilled the beans, it could ruin his life. It would be gratifying to dangle such knowledge over his head every so often and say, "I still might tell." But would Jesus do that?

There will be a payday for those who won't forgive others. "But if you do not forgive others their sins, your Father will not forgive your sins" (Matt. 6:15). God is displeased when you hold another person hostage in fear, especially knowing the things for which you've been forgiven.

You may also seek your revenge by hurting that person's reputation, by keeping others from thinking well of him or her. You might even take the punishment further and administer justice personally, trying to mete out the most severe penalty available. Never mind that God says, "Vengeance is mine!" (Rom. 12:19, KJV). Never mind that God says, "This is something that only I do." If *you* do it, let me make you a promise: it will only be one-tenth of what *God* would have done. If you can't wait on God's timing and His manner, and you say, "I'm going to make sure justice is carried out," God says, "You're on your own."

As we've discussed, forgiveness is a choice you must make, and it is not a choice that comes easily. God knows forgiveness is difficult. It wasn't easy for Jesus to forgive those who put Him to death. It wasn't easy for God to do what He did either, but He did it anyway. He sacrificed His Son, and He asks you to make a little sacrifice in return. You must make the choice to let your enemies off the hook and even *pray* that God will let them off the hook. You must make the choice and live it out. It is an act of the will.

I also believe there's an underlying cause of unforgiveness that many do not realize: we do not put a high enough value on our fellowship with the Father. There should be nothing more important to you than your relationship with God. The apostle John said, "And our fellowship is with the Father and with his Son, Jesus Christ" (1 John 1:3). Do you put a high value on your times of fellowship with the Father? Moreover, does receiving a reward in heaven mean little or nothing to you? If you choose to withhold forgiveness from others, you are not putting a high enough value on things today that one day will mean everything to you.

Here's an even harder truth. John says, "If we claim to have fellowship with him yet walk in the darkness, we lie and do not live by the truth" (1 John 1:6). One way you walk in darkness is by holding bitterness in your heart toward others—bitterness that creates confusion in your mind and oppression in your heart. You may say, "Oh, but I am having fellowship with God." No, you're not. You're just claiming you are having fellowship with God if there is bitterness in your heart. And if you claim to have fellowship with God but walk in darkness, you lie.

Walking in darkness is the consequence of unforgiveness. When I don't forgive, I might spend hours a day in prayer, but I am not having genuine fellowship with God. If I can't forgive the person who hurt someone dear to me, I am walking in darkness. If I can't forgive the person who lied about me to others, I have lost my intimate relationship with the Father. I can even continue to preach, and people might even say, "Oh, what a wonderful sermon! You must be so close to God!" I can sing praises to the Lord with my hands in the air, and you might say, "Oh, look at how R. T. is worshipping the Lord!" I could put on such an act that you would think I am the holiest person in the church. But if I have bitterness inside or am holding a grudge against someone else, I am a liar. I cannot walk in the light when I am really in darkness.

PERSONAL REFLECTION

Have you seen yourself in the description in today's reading? In what ways have resentment and revenge played out in your life?

_____

_____

_____

What do you think God means when He says vengeance is His? Do you think He will give out harsh justice or grant mercy to your enemies? Does it matter?

_____

_____

_____

What does it feel like to walk in darkness? Have you ever felt your prayers were being "blocked" by unforgiveness? How have you gotten out of "darkness" in the past?

_____

_____

_____

DAY 8

Be Honest About Bitterness

WE'VE COME TO our eighth day, and it is time to discuss an inward condition called bitterness. It is an excessive desire for vengeance that comes from deep resentment. It heads the list of things that grieve the Spirit of God (Eph. 4:31). It became Esau's preoccupation. (See Genesis 27:41.) And it is one of the most frequent causes of people missing the grace of God. "See to it that no one falls short of the grace of God and that no bitter root grows up to cause trouble and defile many" (Heb. 12:15). Bitterness will manifest itself in many ways—losing your temper, high blood pressure, irritability, sleeplessness, obsession with getting even, depression, isolation, a constant negative perspective, and generally feeling unwell.

We must therefore begin to get rid of a bitter and unforgiving spirit; otherwise, the attempt to forgive will fail. It is true that doing the right things, even when you don't feel like it, can eventually lead to having the right feelings. In fact if you are able to attempt to do right in this area, it shows that the bitterness is not as deep as it could be. In other words, if someone feels bitter but begins to put the principles of total forgiveness into action, it shows that he or she is not totally controlled by bitterness. Otherwise he or she wouldn't make a start in doing what is right.

The absence of bitterness allows the Holy Spirit to be Himself in you. This means you will become like Jesus. When the Spirit is grieved, you are left to yourself, and you will struggle with emotions ranging from anger to fear. But when the Holy Spirit is not grieved, He is *at home* with you. He will begin to change you into the person He wants you to be, and you will be able to manifest the gentleness of the Spirit. Relinquishing bitterness is an open invitation for the Holy Spirit to give you His peace, His joy, and the knowledge of His will.

This is extremely important when it comes to the matter of reconciliation. Let's say, for example, your best friend has had an affair with your wife. Must you forgive him? Yes. But it does not follow that you will remain closest of friends. If I have totally forgiven the person who has hurt me and I have no bitterness, I should not feel the slightest bit of guilt or shame for not wanting a complete restoration of that relationship. Even if there never had been a friendship in the first place, if someone has greatly wronged me, I can forgive him and yet see it as totally reasonable not to invite him to lunch every Sunday.

The essential factor is that there is no trace of bitterness. How can you be sure that there is no bitterness left in your heart? Bitterness is gone when there is no desire to get even with or punish the offender, when you do or say nothing that would hurt his reputation or future, and when you truly wish him well in all he seeks to do.

PERSONAL REFLECTION

Have you held grudges against anybody for long periods of time? How has this grudge affected your life, your other relationships, your work, and your worship?

_____

_____

_____

_____

_____

Do you now wish this person well, or is there more work to be done in your heart?

_____

_____

_____

_____

_____

DAY 9

Confront Your Critical Spirit

I F LEFT UNDEALT with, the next manifestation of unforgiveness we come to on our forty-day journey is the develop-
ment of a critical spirit. As resentment, bitterness, and a thirst
for revenge become rooted in your spirit, you begin dishing
out criticism of others. It happens so easily. You don't need to
read a book on how to develop a pointing finger. You don't
need more education, a higher IQ, or a lot of experience to
become an expert at criticizing. And it is certainly no sign
that you are more spiritual. It has often been said that a little
bit of learning is a dangerous thing. Sometimes a little bit of
spirituality is a dangerous thing as well because one may be
just spiritual enough to see what is wrong in others—and to
point the finger. The true test of spirituality is being able *not*
to point the finger!

You may say, "Well, I have to say something because
nobody else will!" So what if no one else does? The person
you are criticizing likely doesn't want to hear it, so you are not
really helping anyway. When the person is criticized, he or
she usually will feel bad but won't change his or her behavior.
God's Word is a practical command. "Stop it!" He says.

> If you do away with the yoke of oppression, with
> the pointing finger and malicious talk, and if you
> spend yourselves in behalf of the hungry and satisfy
> the needs of the oppressed, then your light will rise
> in the darkness, and your night will become like the
> noonday.
>
> —ISAIAH 58:9–10

Consider the atmosphere you live in when it is devoid of criticism. How pleasant it is when we all live in harmony (Ps. 133:1). It is so sweet and so good. Now consider the pain that follows when someone is critical of you. When you are criticized, you don't like it because it hurts.

It is harder to say which is more painful: to be falsely accused or truthfully accused. Most of us don't like either situation. But the bottom line is if you don't like being criticized, don't criticize others! A lot of grief could be spared if people would learn to control their tongues.

Paul instructs us, "Let your conversation be always full of grace, seasoned with salt, so that you may know how to answer everyone" (Col. 4:6). Peter adds these words, "Do not repay evil with evil or insult with insult. On the contrary, repay evil with blessing, because to this you were called so that you may inherit a blessing" (1 Pet. 3:9). Jesus Himself even said, "But I tell you that everyone will have to give account on the day of judgment for every empty word they have spoken" (Matt. 12:36). That is enough to scare me into watching what I say!

Uncalled-for criticism usually creates a defensive reaction in the other person that leads to a countercharge. If I accuse you of something, you immediately say, "Yeah, but what about you? I saw you do this; I heard you say that!"

"Oh no I did not!"

"Oh yes you did!"

These conversations are almost always counterproductive. They also grieve the Holy Spirit. When you grieve the Spirit, you lose your presence of mind and your ability to think clearly. You may even lose your self-control.

> The tongue also is a fire, a world of evil among the parts of the body. It corrupts the whole body, sets the whole course of one's life on fire, and is itself set on fire by hell.
>
> —JAMES 3:6

All hell can break loose when you don't learn to control your tongue.

The thing I want you to grasp is that there are two levels of motivation for avoiding a critical spirit. The lower level of motivation is to spare yourself unnecessary trouble. The higher level is to avoid grieving the Holy Spirit; maintain your continual communion with Him, flowing in the Spirit, walking in the Spirit.

If you invite God to become involved in your life, He will. But the very moment you point the finger at another person, He will get involved in a way that you may not like. He may well begin to judge *you*—not them—for doing the judging and criticizing.

As I close today's thoughts, there's one last observation I want to make for you to consider. When you resent another person's getting away with something and escaping punishment, it's often because you are jealous of their situation, that they would be shown mercy when they don't deserve it. Jealousy is one of the hardest things on earth to see in yourself. You can see it in others but never in yourself! You don't want to admit to a fault like that, so you deny it as long as you can. Jealousy sometimes springs from the fear that a person won't get justice. We all want mercy for ourselves but justice for others. I encourage you to take an honest look at yourself and see if jealousy and resentment have been lurking in the corners of your heart, causing you to have a critical spirit. If that is the case, repent and forgive those who have wronged you, and you will be forgiven.

PERSONAL REFLECTION

Think about a good atmosphere you have experienced where there was no ungodly criticism. How can you foster that atmosphere at home? At work? At church?

_____

_____

_____

_____

Are you overly critical of others? Take a moment to ask God to make you less critical of others. Confess any mistakes you have made in recent memory, and ask that you would be able to fully enjoy the forgiveness only God can give.

_____

_____

_____

_____

Stop Playing God

I COULD TAKE YOU to the very spot—a table in the Duke Humphrey wing of the Bodleian Library in Oxford. I was in the process of discovering the works of the great William Perkins (1558–1602), an Elizabethan Puritan. I came in that day feeling very discouraged and inferior compared with the other students at Oxford University. Here I was from the hills of Kentucky, a place not exactly known for its centers of academic excellence. "You don't belong here," my mind suggested—and at that moment my eyes fell on the words of William Perkins:

> Don't believe the devil, even when he tells the truth.

Criticism that is uncalled-for, unfair, or unjust—*even if it is true*—should not be uttered. The fact that what you say is true does not necessarily make it right to say. Often Satan's accusations are true; he is an expert at being a judge. He is even called "the accuser of our brothers and sisters" (Rev. 12:10). You may be pointing your finger and speaking words of truth, but you may unwittingly be an instrument of the devil as you speak.

This kind of uncalled-for criticism is what Jesus means

by judging when He says, "Do not judge." He is not telling us to ignore what is wrong; He is saying not to administer any uncalled-for criticism—that is, criticism that is unfair or unjustified.

The word *judge* comes from the Greek word *krinō*, which basically means "to distinguish."[1] Making a distinction between two things is often a good thing to do. Being discriminate can be prudent, and it can be wise. The apostle Paul said, "The person with the Spirit makes judgments about all things" (1 Cor. 2:15). We are told to make righteous judgments. But what Jesus is talking about here is judging *people* and unfairly criticizing them. It is our way of playing God.

One acrostic I have found helpful is built on the word NEED. When speaking to or about another person, ask yourself if what you are about to say will meet the person's need.

> Necessary—Is it necessary to say this?
>
> Encourage—Will this encourage the person? Will it make him or her feel better?
>
> Edify—Will it edify? Will what you say build the person up and make him or her stronger?
>
> Dignify—Will it dignify that person? Jesus treated other people with a sense of dignity.

For years I have read Luke 6:37 every day; it says, "Do not judge, and you will not be judged." I made the decision many years ago to read it every day, and I still do. Every single day. Why have I chosen this particular verse to focus on? Because judging is probably my greatest weakness.

Judging other people is almost always counterproductive. When I judge someone else, I may be thinking, "What I

want to do is change this person, straighten this person out."
But it has the opposite effect almost every time! Sooner or
later it will backfire. The other person will become offended,
and the situation will not be resolved.

The degree to which we resist the temptation to judge
will be the degree to which we ourselves are largely spared
of being judged: "Do not judge, or you too will be judged"
(Matt. 7:1) In Matthew this statement is given as a warning,
but in Luke it is given as a promise.

> Do not judge, and you will not be judged. Do not
> condemn, and you will not be condemned. Forgive,
> and you will be forgiven.
>
> —LUKE 6:37

Judging people is the next result of unforgiveness, and it
entails elbowing in on God's exclusive territory. Deuteronomy
32:35 ("It is mine to avenge; I will repay") is quoted twice in
the New Testament (Rom. 12:19; Heb. 10:30). That means
it's not *your* job! Judging is God's prerogative, nobody else's.
To move in on the territory of the eternal judge will get His
attention—but not the kind of attention you want!

The word *godliness* means being like God, and there are
certain aspects of God's character that He commands you to
imitate. For example, you are commanded to live a holy life
(1 Pet. 1:16). You are commanded to show mercy (Luke 6:36).
God wants you to walk in integrity. He wants you to walk in
truth and sincerity. But there is an aspect of the character of
God where there is *no trespassing allowed*, and the moment
you begin to point your finger at other people, you are on it—
you are sinning. That aspect is being a judge.

If you and I are foolish enough to administer uncalled-for
criticism, we should remember three things:

- God is listening.

- He knows the truth about us.

- He is ruthlessly fair.

Never forget that God knows the truth about you, as Malachi says.

> Then those who feared the LORD talked with each other, and the LORD listened and heard. A scroll of remembrance was written in his presence concerning those who feared the LORD and honored his name.
> —MALACHI 3:16

How would you like it if, as you are pointing the finger at someone else, an angel from heaven showed up and said, "Stop! Here's what I know about *you*," and then he revealed your secret sins to the person you were judging?

God has a way of exposing people just when they begin to think, "There is no way that could happen to me." The Lord promises that equitable judgment will be administered. The word *equitable* means fair or just. All of God's judgments are ruthlessly fair.

At the judgment seat of Christ, before which you will stand one day, God's judgment of your life will be fair. But God also deals with people in this present life, especially if they are saved. He doesn't always wait for the final judgment to begin disciplining His children.

Read Matthew 7, and you'll realize that Jesus will not allow you to play God. He is the ultimate judge, and you must be extremely careful not to trespass into His territory.

PERSONAL REFLECTION

Have you ever been judged wrongly? How did it feel? Did it help you along in your faith walk or stall you?

_____

_____

_____

_____

_____

Have you ever judged someone wrongly? Think about the situation and the result. Has God ever dealt with you harshly as a result of your judgmental attitude?

_____

_____

_____

_____

_____

When You Can—and
Can't—Help Others

WHEN YOU READ the strong language of Matthew 7:1, "Do not judge, or you too will be judged," it might be easy to conclude that there is *never* a situation in which you should make a judgment regarding another person. But this is not the case. When Jesus goes on to say, "First take the plank out of your own eye, and then you will see clearly to remove the speck from your brother's eye" (v. 5), He is not denying that there will be times in which you should help to remove the "specks" from the eyes of your brothers.

Sometimes it is right to warn others about someone's behavior. For example, the apostle John, who has so much to say about loving one another, warned about a troublemaker in the church. (See 3 John 9–10.) Paul reported that Demas had forsaken him because he "loved this world" and said that Alexander the metalworker had caused him "a great deal of harm" (2 Tim. 4:10, 14). But referring to all who had deserted him, Paul advised, "May it not be held against them" (v. 16).

It is an injustice when people who have done and can still do great harm to others remain at large. This is why a person who is raped should testify in court; it is why a person who threatens the unity of the church should be dealt with. But basic principles must be followed in this type of judgment that allow justice to be carried out without violating total forgiveness.

Jesus' rhetorical question "Why do you look at the speck of sawdust in your brother's eye and pay no attention to the plank in your own eye?" (Matt. 7:3) confronts the tendency to meddle over what gets your goat. Faultfinding is out of order. The fault you see in someone else is what Jesus calls a "speck"—a little thing that annoys you. But the whole time you overlook your own very serious problems, the "plank," or beam, in your own eye.

Jesus wants you to see that you have a serious problem when you are critical and point the finger. The act of faultfinding is worse than the fault you think you see in the other person. Before Jesus provides instruction about making a correction in another person, He establishes the criterion for being qualified as a judge: you must look objectively at yourself.

So, then, is Jesus telling you that you can be qualified to judge after all? Yes, sometimes you are. If you are able to remove the plank from your own eyes, you are apparently set free to remove the speck from another's eye.

But who would be bold enough to say that he or she has no plank? I am certainly not that bold. If I must know that there is no plank in my eye before I can offer any sort of correction to or warning about an evil person, I am out of the picture! I will never be qualified to judge.

The words of Matthew 7:5 are intended to help you in the difficult situations you confront in life and bring a balance between a godly, forgiving spirit and an attitude of judgmentalism. The principles of total forgiveness must be practiced with balance and common sense.

- Jesus wants you to be honest with Him and with yourself. Admit that you are unqualified as a judge as long as there is a plank in your eye. (And realize that we all have planks in our eyes at one time or another.)

- Jesus also wants to promote humility. It would be the height of arrogance to claim you have completely gotten rid of your plank.

- Jesus wants you to move forward, past the offense into a lifestyle of forgiveness. Jesus also wants you to extend your help to others. But He never says you should not see what is very clearly there.

- Jesus is promoting honesty and humility, but He is also showing you what to do in certain situations where things have gone wrong—situations in which someone needs to speak out against sin or injustice and it would be irresponsible not to do so.

A closer look at Jesus' words shows you the order in which you should place your priorities: "First, take the plank out of your own eye." If you want to help a person in need or speak up against an injustice, your first priority must be to get things right in your own heart. This means to admit humbly and soberly your own weaknesses.

When Jesus asks you to remove the plank from your own eye, He is telling you to disqualify yourself if you get upset with the one who has a speck! You are qualified to help another person only to the extent that you truly love and care for him or her.

Follow this rule of thumb: the one who is hardest on

himself or herself will probably be the gentlest with others. Those who are most aware of their own weaknesses are most likely to be able to help others. Those qualified to remove the speck of dust are impartial and will not moralize, make the person feel guilty, or be governed by any personal interest. Their only consideration will be the honor of God's name.

When You *Can't* Help Another

To summarize today's portion, Jesus has provided some objective principles to follow when determining when it is right and wrong to judge. You should rule yourself out when:

- Your nose is out of joint because something or someone has gotten your goat. In other words, when you are churned up, stay out.

- You are personally or emotionally involved. Even if an injustice has been committed, you should stay out of the situation—unless you have specifically been asked to testify or give your opinion.

- Your desire is to punish or get even.

- There is envy or jealousy in your heart.

- Your own self-esteem is related.

When You *Can* Help Another

You are able to help when:

- You are meeting a need. (To refresh your memory on this, here is the NEED acrostic I mentioned on day 10.)

  Necessary—Is it necessary to say this?

Encourage—Will this encourage the person? Will it make him or her feel better?

Edify—Will it edify? Will what you say build the person up and make him or her stronger?

Dignify—Will it dignify that person? Jesus treated other people with a sense of dignity.

- You would be irresponsible not to speak out. It is appropriate to get involved if you are in a strategic position to help.

- You have been asked to step in by a responsible person who has no agenda.

- You are utterly impartial and have no agitation or feeling of being annoyed.

- Nothing matters to you more than the honor of God. Be careful! Many meddlers use this as their justification. One day you will find out whether it really was God's honor you cared about—or just your own!

PERSONAL REFLECTION

Think of an example of a "plank" you might have in your own eye. Now think of an example of a "speck" in someone else's. Are you a professional "speck hunter"? Why is it so tempting to point out specks while ignoring your planks?

_____

_____

_____

_____

_____

_____

_____

_____

Have you ever seen someone restored by gentle correction or confrontation? Pause and ask God for wisdom in this area, as someday you may be called upon to correct or confront a brother or sister in Christ.

_____

_____

_____

_____

_____

_____

_____

_____

Day 12

The Choice Is Yours

SCRIPTURES SUCH AS Ephesians 4:32 and Colossians 3:13 reveal that God has given a mandate in His Word regarding forgiveness. So what happens if you choose not to forgive? Although you are *saved* by grace alone, there remain consequences if you choose to walk in unforgiveness. Some aspects of your relationship with God are unchangeable, but others are affected by the things you do.

- Salvation is unconditional; fellowship with the Father is conditional.

- Justification before God is unconditional; the anointing of the Spirit is conditional.

- Your status in the family of God is unconditional; your intimacy with Christ is conditional.

If you choose not to forgive others, it will affect your fellowship with God, it will hinder your intimacy with Christ, and it will grieve the Holy Spirit. Perhaps this is why God hates an unforgiving spirit so much.

I also believe God hates unforgiveness because in order

to forgive you and me, He paid a severe price. I predict that when you get to heaven, you will be able to see, little by little, what it meant for God to send His Son to die on a cross. God did for you what you did not deserve. He therefore wants you to pass this on to others who don't deserve it.

God loves reconciliation. He has given the ministry of reconciliation to you, and He wants it to continue. When you are forgiven, He wants you to pass it on. When you interrupt that, He doesn't like it at all. He sent His Son to die on a cross, effectually calling you by His grace and giving you total forgiveness. But you interrupt that flow by not passing it on.

God knows the sins for which He has forgiven you. He knows all that you have done, the things that no one else will ever hear about. If you turn around and say, "I can't forgive that person for what he has done," God doesn't like it at all. He considers that ingratitude, and He hates it.

The mistake many make is saying openly and (seemingly) reasonably, "I know I am a sinner. I have done some pretty horrible things—but not as bad and horrible as that which they have done to me." This is a most common line, whether it is rape, child abuse, vicious lying, or infidelity. You might say, "I would never rape, murder, or physically abuse anybody." Or you might say, "I may have stolen from that convenience store. I may have cheated on my income tax. I may even have gossiped a little. But I would never abuse a child." You might be among those who say, "I know what it is to lose my temper. I have been jealous at times. I have coveted someone else's success. But I've never done anything so wicked as to be unfaithful to my beloved spouse."

I understand this. You might have to forgive specific wrongs that you yourself would never do to another. But what you don't realize at first—and the truth may not be faced for a long time—is the meaning of Jesus' words that those who are unjust in small matters will also be unjust in large matters (Luke 16:10). Agree or disagree, that is Jesus' doctrine of sin. That is His view of people. The "little" sins you do that seem relatively harmless (taking a ballpoint pen from the office) only show what else you would do if you knew you would get away with it.

The point is this: God knows not only the sins you have committed but also the sins of which you are capable. He knows your heart. He sees what is deep down inside that you may not be willing to face. Your self-righteousness and personal sense of decency often camouflage the evil that is within your soul. When the Bible says in 1 John 1:7 that Jesus' blood purifies from *all sin*, it means you have been forgiven even for sins you weren't aware of.

The truth is that given the right circumstances, pressure, temptation, and timing, *any* of us can match the evil (or its equivalent in God's sight) we ourselves have to forgive. If we deny this, it is because we don't agree with what the Bible says about men and women of any color, culture, education, or background.

And yet agreeing with the Bible doesn't make it easy. You might still be indignant that this person—who knows the truth and should have known better—could carry out this deed or hurt you like that. But the Bible is saying that:

- You are guilty of a different sin that is just as heinous in God's eyes.

- You are capable of a sin just as bad in God's eyes.

- You may yet fall into such a sin as they did—or worse.

Not forgiving leads not only to deeper bitterness but also to the capability of enacting a wrong that is worse than you ever dreamed of doing. God *could* judge you by allowing you eventually to fall into the exact same sin that you are required to forgive, should you dig your heels in and remain recalcitrant. I have certainly seen it happen. I know of people who were indignant over a particular conduct but later did the very thing they criticized. This is why Jesus said, "Do not judge, or you too will be judged" (Matt. 7:1).

Making a choice to continue in unforgiveness shows that you aren't sufficiently grateful for God's forgiveness of your own sins. Perhaps you haven't taken seriously enough your own sin or your own redemption. Probably what you want to say is, "Well, what I did wasn't nearly as bad as what they have done!" And that's where you are wrong! God hates self-righteousness as much as He hates the injustice that you think is so horrible, and He certainly doesn't like it when you judge. So if you must forget the sins of which God has forgiven you, at least remember that one of the most heinous sins of all is self-righteousness. (But realize this: as much as God hates self-righteousness, He will forgive you of that sin too!)

When you understand the magnitude of your sins that God has forgiven, you cannot help but be grateful for what He has done, and it becomes easy to forgive other people. Have you overlooked the sin of self-righteousness in your own heart? Have you forgotten how much you need God's forgiveness? If you honestly examine what's in your heart, it should cause you to have a new appreciation for the forgiveness you've received and a new perspective on granting that same forgiveness to others.

PERSONAL REFLECTION

Recall the time when you received your first lesson on giving or receiving forgiveness. What did you learn from it? How do you define *forgiveness*?

_____

_____

_____

_____

What types of offenses do you find hardest to forgive (personal betrayal, a loved one's forgetfulness/carelessness, a loved one's anger, being overlooked, being cheated, offenses involving money, offenses involving your children, etc.)? Which offenses do you find easiest to forgive?

_____

_____

_____

_____

_____

Whom Do You Need to Forgive?

"Forgive Us ... as We Also Have Forgiven"

SINCE FORGIVENESS IS a choice, what's next? As we begin section 3 of our journey today, I trust you have been persuaded that forgiveness is the right choice and have decided to do it and not look back. In this section of our journey we will explore the various people you might need to forgive. It starts with an understanding of the Lord's Prayer.

I suppose that the fifth petition of the Lord's Prayer, "Forgive us our debts, as we also have forgiven our debtors" (Matt. 6:12), has made liars out of more people than any other line in human history. But don't blame Jesus for that. We should mean what we say if we choose to pray the Lord's Prayer. And Jesus did not say we had a choice; He said, "This, then, is how you should pray" (v. 9).

"Forgive us our debts" is obviously a plea for forgiveness from God. But then comes the following line (or possibly the big lie): "as we also have forgiven our debtors." This petition is both a plea for forgiveness and a claim that we have already forgiven those who hurt us. In Luke's version of the account Jesus says, "Forgive us our sins, for we also forgive everyone who sins against us" (Luke 11:4). There the verb *forgive* is in the present tense; when we pray in that manner, we are claiming that we are forgiving everyone.

When you pray this petition, you are asking God to forgive all your sins. This line, however, is not a prayer for salvation. It is not what we call the "sinner's prayer," which is essentially the way a person comes to Christ. (See Luke 18:13.) On the contrary, these words constitute a prayer that only a believer—one who can truly call God "Father"—can pray.

What, then, is the purpose of this prayer? It is not to appeal to our own strength but to keep us in fellowship with the Father. In order to have fellowship with the Father, because God is light and in Him there is no darkness at all (1 John 1:5), all our sin must be cleansed. Walking in the light means following without compromise *anything God shows you to do*. But if He shows you something and you sweep it under the carpet, years later you will wonder why you haven't grown spiritually. The reason will be because you postponed obedience; there was no real fellowship with the Father.

The Lord's Prayer is designed to keep us from having a self-righteous attitude. We all have this problem, and most of us fight it every day. We naturally want to justify ourselves; we instinctively want to point the finger. This prayer helps to keep us on our toes spiritually and gives us objectivity about ourselves. This prayer shows us that we need daily forgiveness as much as we need daily bread.

There are two things Jesus takes for granted in the Lord's Prayer: that people have hurt us and that we ourselves will need to be forgiven. We have all come short of God's glory, and often other people come short of treating us with the dignity, love, and respect that we would like. We have hurt God, and we want to be let off the hook; people have hurt us, and we must let them off the hook.

In what ways have you been hurt by other people? Perhaps you have been discredited or dishonored; maybe you have been disappointed that people could be so ungrateful. You may have been lied about or taken advantage of; people may not have been very appreciative; they may have been disloyal. Think of someone in your life who has discredited you. Think of someone in your life who has disappointed you because he or she was not grateful. Jesus is telling us that's the way people are.

You may not realize it, but you do the same thing to other people. Wouldn't you like them to let *you* off the hook? You pray that God won't throw the book at you, and yet you pray that God will throw the book at them.

Do you want God to let *you* off the hook? As I previously mentioned, we all have skeletons in our closets. What if God decided that because you refused to forgive another person, He would pull a skeleton out of your closet and let everyone else know what He knows about you? That is a pretty good motivation, if you ask me, to say, "God, forgive them. Yes, thank You very much. Please forgive them."

Not only do we need daily forgiveness as much as we need daily bread, but we also need to pray daily that we have the grace to forgive others as a lifelong commitment. It is not easy. No one ever said it would be. It has been the hardest thing I have ever had to do, but following this phrase in the Lord's Prayer is the clearest path to fellowship with God.

As soon as Jesus finished teaching His disciples the Lord's Prayer, He made another remark.

> For if you forgive other people when they sin against you, your heavenly Father will also forgive you.
> —Matthew 6:14

It is as though Jesus added a P.S. to the Lord's Prayer: "For *if* you forgive men when they sin against you, your heavenly

Father will also forgive you." Why does Jesus add this further statement? The most natural tendency in the world is to want to get even when someone has offended you. It is as natural as eating or sleeping, and it is instinctual. Jesus is telling us to do something that is not natural but supernatural: totally forgiving people—sometimes those closest to us—for the wrongs they do to us.

The kingdom of heaven is the domain of the Holy Spirit. When the Holy Spirit is at home in us, it means He is not grieved. He can be Himself; He isn't adjusting to us, but we are adjusting to Him. When Jesus said, "If you forgive other people when they sin against you, your heavenly Father will also forgive you," He was referring to receiving the anointing of God and participating in an intimate relationship with the Father. Unless we are walking in a state of forgiveness toward others, we cannot be in an intimate relationship with God.

PERSONAL REFLECTION

Looking back, can you think of a time when a lack of forgiveness on your part has led to a detour in your spiritual walk? Are you still in that place of stagnation now?

_____

_____

_____

_____

_____

_____

_____

_____

_____

Ask the Holy Spirit to shine His light on any area of unforgiveness in your heart that is hindering your spiritual growth
and intimacy with God. Repent today. Forgive, and you will
be forgiven, and you will experience renewed fellowship with
your heavenly Father.

_____

_____

_____

_____

_____

_____

_____

_____

Day 14

Forgiving Your Enemies

WHAT IS AN enemy? It is a person who either wants to harm you or who would say something about you so as to call your credibility or integrity into question. The person would rejoice at your downfall or lack of success. He or she would not pray that God would bless you and prosper you but instead would sincerely hope that God would bring you down.

An enemy is a person who hates you but would never admit to the word *hate*. I say that because should your enemy be a Christian, he or she knows it is wrong to hate. So the person will use any other word or phrase: "loathe," "despise," "I just can't stand them," "They make me sick," or "I can't stand the sight of them." In other words, the person just doesn't like you and will show it one way or another sooner or later.

An enemy is also a person who will take unfair advantage of you; he or she will "despitefully use you" (Matt. 5:44, KJV). The person will walk all over you. If he or she knows you place vengeance in God's hands rather than your own, instead of respecting this, the person will exploit it all the more—knowing you will not retaliate. Sometimes a Christian will be unscrupulous in business with another believer, knowing this particular Christian would never take

him or her to court. (See 1 Corinthians 6:1–8.) This person
may say libelous things in print, knowing you will not sue.

An enemy will often persecute you. The Greek word for
persecute simply means to follow or to pursue. Enemies will
pursue you because they are obsessed with you. King Saul
became jealous of David because he had become more popular,
and King Saul was more worried about the threat of David's
anointing than he was of Israel's archenemy—the Philistines!
Saul pursued David, but he never succeeded in killing him.

The persecutor's main tactic is to discredit you. This person
will speak badly about you to your boss, keeping you from getting that promotion or raise in pay; tell your friends about any
indiscretions he or she might perceive in your life; and go out
of his or her way to keep you from succeeding and from being
admired by the people in the office or at church. What is
more, Christians in the role of persecutors may deceive themselves into thinking that they are doing it for God and His
glory! "They will put you out of the synagogue; in fact, a time
is coming when anyone who kills you will think he is offering
a service to God" (John 16:2). Persecutors don't kill with the
sword or a gun; they do it with the tongue or pen. Perhaps
sometimes you wish they would just physically kill you and
get it over with!

THE BLESSING OF HAVING AN ENEMY

When you know that a person is obsessed with you and is
out to discredit you, you are very, very blessed indeed. This
doesn't happen to everyone. You are chosen, for behind your
enemy is the hand of God. God has raised up your enemy—
possibly just for you! King Saul's pursuit of David was the
best thing that could have happened to David at the time.
It was a part—a most vital part—of David's preparation to

become king. He had the anointing (1 Sam. 16:13) without the crown, and God was ensuring that when the day came for him to wear the crown, he would be ready. Dr. Martyn Lloyd-Jones used to say to me: "The worst thing that can happen to a man is to succeed before he is ready." God did David a very special favor: He raised up Saul to keep David on his toes, to teach him to be sensitive to the Spirit (see 1 Samuel 24:5), and to teach him total forgiveness. Saul was David's passport to a greater anointing.

If you have a real, relentless, genuine enemy—someone who is not a figment of your anxiety or imagination—you should see yourself as sitting on a mine of twenty-four-carat gold. Not everybody is that blessed! But if you have been blessed in that way, take it with both hands. You should take this person's picture, enlarge it, frame it, and thank God every time you look at it. Your enemy, should you handle him or her correctly, could turn out to be the best thing that ever happened to you.

While I was writing *Total Forgiveness*, I related an incident that led to my having to forgive those who hurt me many years ago. I've even told my wife, Louise, that it was "the best thing that ever happened to me." Perhaps that is a *slight* exaggeration when I think of all the other wonderful things that have happened to me—my conversion and my marriage to Louise being the top two. But that is often the way I feel; I wouldn't take *anything* in exchange for the devastating incident that led me to that new understanding of how to totally forgive.

TOTALLY FORGIVING YOUR ENEMIES

When you totally forgive your enemy, you have crossed over into the supernatural realm. Perhaps you are like me and wish you could excel in all the gifts of the Spirit; you wish you could have a hand in signs and wonders; you'd love to see your usefulness intensified and extended by a double anointing. The gifts are *supernatural*; that is, they are above and beyond the natural order of things. There is no natural explanation for the truly miraculous. But if you and I totally forgive one who is truly an enemy, believe me, we have just crossed over into the realm of the supernatural.

You may not speak in tongues; you may not have raised a person from the dead. But when you totally forgive an authentic enemy, you are *there*; you have made it into the big leagues.

I believe we are talking about the highest level of spirituality that exists. This is as good as it gets. Totally forgiving an enemy is as spectacular as any miracle. No one may even know, though. You quietly intercede for the person in solitude. Only God, the angels, and the devil know.

We are talking about a feat greater than climbing Mount Everest, for totally forgiving an enemy is climbing the spiritual Everest. It means the highest watermark in anyone's spiritual pilgrimage.

And yet it is within reach of any of us. No high connections in government, business, or society are required. No particular cultural background is needed. No university education is needed. A high level of intelligence is not required. You and I can do something exceedingly rare: forgive an enemy (if we have one). Loving an enemy defies natural explanation.

It begins with having sufficient motivation. I am literally seeking to motivate you in these lines to do what very few do—but what all *can* do: totally forgive anyone who has hurt you. And the blessing is beyond words to describe.

66 | 40 Days to Total Forgiveness

PERSONAL REFLECTION

Do you have known enemies? What have they done to prove
they are your enemies? Characterize your response and relationship to these people thus far. How do you intend to
change your response to them now?

_____

_____

_____

_____

_____

What does it feel like to cross over into that supernatural
realm of total forgiveness? Do you think you are there now?

_____

_____

_____

_____

_____

_____

Beyond Forgiveness: *Loving* Your Enemies

JESUS PUTS TO us the greatest challenge that ever was—a greater challenge to the human spirit than science faced in putting a man on the moon. It is simply to love your enemy. Jesus uses the word *agape*, as Paul did in 1 Corinthians 13. It is not *eros* (physical or sexual love), nor is it *phileo* (brotherly love). *Agape* is *selfless concern for others*. It is self-giving love. Agape is not necessarily affection. You may love (agape) a person and not like him or her. You may love a person and not want to spend a holiday with him or her. You can love a person and act selfishly toward that person.

This challenge can be almost overwhelming. Jesus instructs us to overcome our enemy, not by showing everybody how wrong he or she was or by matching his or her hatred with ours but by loving the person.

This brings us back to the matter of choice. Love is not what you feel. Forgiving is not doing what comes naturally. It is often said, "You can't help what you feel." We therefore ask, Does the choice to love involve repressing or denying our feelings? No. Repression is almost never a good thing to do. But love is a conscious choice to forgive—even if you don't feel like it! If you wait until you feel like it, you probably never will forgive. You must do it because it is right, because of a choice you have made that is not based on your feelings.

Nelson Mandela had been asked many times how he emerged from all those years in prison without being bitter. His reply was simple: "As I walked out the door toward the gate that would lead to my freedom, I knew if I didn't leave my bitterness and hatred behind, I'd still be in prison."[1] Oddly many who are bitter fully realize this, yet they still can't forgive. They rationally understand that bitterness is self-impoverishing, but they continue to harbor it. How did Mandela overcome his feelings? The answer can be found in his own words: "I realized that they could take everything from me except my mind and my heart. They could not take those things. Those things I still had control over. And I decided not to give them away."[2]

The paradox in total forgiveness is that it simultaneously involves selfishness and unselfishness. It is selfish in that you do not want to hurt yourself by holding on to bitterness, and it is unselfish in that you commit yourself to the well-being of your enemy! You could almost say that total forgiveness is both extreme selfishness and extreme unselfishness. You are looking out for your own interests when you totally forgive, but you are also totally setting your offender free.

Even the non-Christian understands the benefits of forgiveness in a physical and emotional sense. This surely leaves all of us without excuse. If a non-Christian is able to forgive others, how much more should the Christian follow a lifestyle of forgiveness? We are the ones who have been warned by Jesus.

> For if you forgive other people when they sin against
> you, your heavenly Father will also forgive you. But

if you do not forgive others their sins, your Father
will not forgive your sin.

—Matthew 6:14–15

As Christians we have no choice. We forfeit our fellowship
with God and blessings here below when we don't forgive. If
we have been forgiven of all our sins—and this includes even
the sins we have forgotten about—how dare we withhold this
from others?

PERSONAL REFLECTION

Before moving on, write a prayer asking God to bless anyone
who has behaved like an enemy toward you—a rude clerk at
the store, an aggressive driver, someone at work or church who
opposes you for some reason, or even a family member who
is out to get you. In your prayer thank God for this blessing!

_____

_____

_____

_____

_____

_____

DAY 16

Forgiving Your Friends

NOT EVERYONE WE must forgive is an enemy. There are those we must forgive who either do not know they have hurt us or if they do, would never have done so intentionally. But we must forgive anyone toward whom we feel anger because it is we, not they, who are in need of healing. That is why total forgiveness—in a sense—becomes a selfish thing.

Some of the people I have had to forgive the most were not my enemies at all. By this I mean that they were not trying to bring me down or hurt me. They were people I had hoped would help me. On one occasion I asked an old friend to write a commendation for a book I had written. He refused, partly because there wasn't enough in it he agreed with and partly because I was gaining a reputation for mixing with people of whom he didn't approve. This hurt. He was no enemy, but I had to forgive him. I have had to forgive those who felt a need to distance themselves from me because I don't echo their "party line." I have had to forgive those who no longer need me as they once did. All these things hurt. The irony is that it is sometimes harder to forgive those who are not enemies but who have hurt you deeply than it is to forgive one who is indeed an enemy.

I do believe I have had some enemies in my life—people not only who were opposed to me and my teaching but who actively sought to bring me down and destroy my reputation. I have had to forgive them—totally—and I believe that by the grace of God I truly have.

The greater the hurt, the greater the blessing that will come with forgiveness. The chief motivation to forgive is not only the promise of mercy that will be extended to us but also the greater reward that is promised—whether it be bestowed here below or in heaven. Jesus confirmed this when He spoke of the ultimate beatitude.

> Blessed are you when people insult you, persecute you and falsely say all kinds of evil against you because of me. Rejoice and be glad, because great is your reward in heaven, for in the same way they persecuted the prophets who were before you.
> —MATTHEW 5:11–12

Jesus tenderly shows us in the Lord's Prayer that we will be hurt—and by people we never dreamed would hurt us. We might think, "Well, yes, I can imagine so-and-so hurting me, but I never thought it would be you!" Psalm 41:9 candidly predicts what Jesus warns us of: "Even my close friend, whom I trusted, he who shared my bread, has lifted up his heel against me" (bsb). We will be hurt by the people we love. What's more, Jesus calls the acts that they do against us "sin."

When people don't mean to hurt

Now, there is more than one kind of wound that causes hurt and pain. In some cases people disappoint you by doing things they think are necessary. They don't intend to hurt you, but they do. As a parent or church leader you sometimes do this—you must make a decision and then say, "I'm sorry, but this is the way it has to be."

People in my life have made these kinds of decisions. Even though wounding me was not their motive, they knew their decisions would hurt me, and they did. In these cases the offense is not an outright sin you must forgive, but you are hurt nonetheless.

Hurt caused by insensitivity

On the other hand, there are people in our world whose actions are called "sin." And again, there is more than one kind of such sin. There are sins that are not willfully committed but nonetheless are done without any sensitivity toward the feelings of others. A person can be so full of himself—due to his own anger or ambition—that he hurts other people without realizing it. Never forget that you might have hurt others unwittingly; we all sin every day, and we therefore should pray daily for those we have hurt without even knowing it.

We must learn to foster a spirit of sensitivity to those around us. The more sensitive I am to the Holy Spirit, the more aware I will be of people around me who are in pain. Remember the words written about Jesus: "A bruised reed he will not break" (Matt. 12:20). I want to treat every single person I meet in that manner, but I fear I do not always do that. So there is one kind of sin where the offenders are not malicious, they are not hateful, and their motive is not to hurt, but they still sin through their insensitivity to others.

Hurt caused by sins knowingly committed

But there are also sins that are willfully committed. Some people do wicked things with their eyes wide open, and these people surely have to know they have done something wrong.

You may say, "Do I have to forgive even that?" The answer is yes.

There is a wonderful consolation, however: the greater the sin you must forgive, the greater the measure of the Spirit that will come to you. So if you have an extremely difficult situation on your hands and you say, "I can't forgive this!" you may not realize at first that there, handed to you on a silver platter, is an opportunity to receive a measure of anointing that someone else might not ever get! Consider it a challenge and an opportunity; take it with both hands. Welcome the opportunity to forgive the deepest hurt, the greatest injustice, and remember that a greater anointing is waiting for you.

What sin is it that we must forgive? Any sin that has been committed against us. We must begin by not judging. It is not for us to judge another's motives. Reserving judgment for God alone shows that we are already beginning to forgive. We must leave to God how guilty our offenders are before Him. We may not know whether what they did was deliberate; we can only know for certain that we were hurt. It may be that our offenders are the way they are because of bad parenting when they were children. I am sure that all our children sooner or later will realize where we as parents have failed and will need to forgive us. I have had to forgive my dad for his imperfections. Perhaps you have had to forgive that unfair schoolteacher, that incompetent boss. Moreover, you must also forgive a fellow Christian who has been insensitive.

Jesus is talking about a chosen privilege: "If you forgive men"—that is, if you *choose* to do it. You can choose not to. "A person's wisdom yields patience; it is to one's glory to overlook an offense" (Prov. 19:11). Can you think of many other things that can bring glory? Winning a gold medal in the Olympics? Winning the Nobel Peace Prize? That may be glory, but Proverbs 19:11 says, "It is to one's glory to overlook an offense." That is far more spectacular in God's eyes than winning any Olympic competition. It is glory *to overlook an offense*.

PERSONAL REFLECTION

Think of friends you have had to forgive. Was it harder to forgive them than to forgive an "enemy"? Is it possible to have friendships without hurting or being hurt? How specifically can you be a more forgiving friend?

_____

_____

_____

_____

_____

Make a mental list of the people in your life who have not disappointed you at one time or another. How long is the list? Did even one person make it? Now think about how you have learned to deal with disappointments. Be honest. Don't just tell yourself what you wish were true.

_____

_____

_____

_____

_____

Think about a time when someone unintentionally hurt you. How did you resolve it in your heart? Do you consider yourself a sensitive person? What are the benefits and drawbacks of being sensitive? Of being insensitive?

_____

_____

_____

_____

Now think about the biggest injustice you've ever had to forgive. How long did it take for you to "perfect" forgiveness, or are you still working on it?

_____

_____

_____

_____

_____

DAY 17

Forgiving Yourself

TOTAL FORGIVENESS MEANS forgiving people—totally—and also forgiving God. But it also must include the total forgiveness of ourselves.

One common complaint every church leader hears is this: "I know God forgives me, but I just can't seem to forgive myself." This is such an important concept that we will discuss it further later in the book. But I must say here and now: there is no lasting joy in forgiveness if it doesn't include forgiving yourself. It is anything but *total* forgiveness if we forgive God and those who hurt us but we are unable to forgive ourselves. It is as wrong as not forgiving others, because God loves us just as much as He loves others; He will be just as unhappy when we don't forgive ourselves as when we hold a grudge against others. Put simply, we matter to God. He wants our lives to be filled with joy. He not only wants us to forgive ourselves, but He also wants it urgently.

Total forgiveness brings such joy and satisfaction that I am almost tempted to call it a selfish enterprise. As we have seen, the wider research that is taking place these days has already overwhelmingly concluded that the first person to experience delight when forgiveness takes place is the one who forgives.

I pray that what has been written and what follows will

challenge and motivate you to forgive those who have hurt you, to forgive the God who let it happen, and to forgive yourself—totally.

FORGIVING OURSELVES

Forgiving ourselves means experiencing the love that keeps no record of our *own* wrongs. This love is a choice, as we have seen, and crossing over to the place where we choose to forgive ourselves is no small step.

It is one thing to have this breakthrough regarding others—totally forgiving them and destroying the record of their wrongs; it is quite another to experience the greater breakthrough—total forgiveness of ourselves.

So many Christians say, "I can forgive others, but how can I ever forget what I have done? I know God forgives me, but I can't forgive myself."

We must remember that forgiving ourselves is also a life-long commitment. In precisely the same way that I must forgive others every single day—which is why I read Luke 6:37 daily—I must also forgive myself.

Forgiving others is a lifelong commitment because:

- We are so often made to relive the wrong committed against us.

- We may feel irked that the offender is getting away with it—forever.

- Satan moves in to exploit our weakness in this area.

This is why we must *renew* our commitment to forgive each and every day—and be sure we haven't pasted together those torn-up bits of paper we once used to record the wrongs done to us.

Forgiving ourselves is also a daily process. We may wake up each day with the awareness of past mistakes and failures and fervently wish that we could turn the clock back and start all over. We may have feelings of guilt, or *pseudoguilt*, if our sins have been placed under the blood of Christ. But the enemy, the devil, loves to move in and take advantage of our thoughts. That is why forgiving ourselves is as important as forgiving an enemy.

Forgiving yourself may bring about the breakthrough you have been looking for. It could set you free in ways you have never before experienced. This is because you have been afraid to forgive yourself. You cling to fear as if it were a thing of value. The truth is, this kind of fear is no friend but rather a fierce enemy. The very breath of Satan is behind the fear of forgiving yourself.

Jesus knows that many of us have this problem. This is a further reason Jesus turned up unexpectedly after His resurrection where, behind closed doors, the disciples were assembled both in terror and in guilt. Not only did Jesus want them to know they were totally forgiven; He also wanted them to forgive themselves. Instead of reminding them of what they had done, He spoke to them as if nothing had happened. He said, "As the Father has sent me, I am sending you" (John 20:21). This gave them dignity. It showed them that nothing had occurred that would change Jesus' plans and strategy for them. He had already sent a signal to Peter, who had denied knowing Jesus, through the angel who said, "But go, tell his disciples and Peter, 'He is going ahead of you into Galilee. There you will see him, just as he told you'" (Mark 16:7). And yet all of them had "deserted him and fled" (Matt.

26:56). After His crucifixion, they felt utterly unworthy. And then the risen Lord showed up and assured them of a future ministry!

I have often thought that one of the reasons Peter was so effective on the day of Pentecost is that he was keenly aware of having been forgiven. He knew full well that just a few weeks before, he had denied Jesus to a little servant girl! He would never forget the look on Jesus' face when the rooster crowed and Peter "went outside and wept bitterly" (Luke 22:61–62). It was a real antidote to self-righteousness! When Peter preached to his fellow Jews on the day of Pentecost, there was no trace of smugness or condescension. Knowing he was a forgiven sinner also kept him from usurping God's glory on that day. God alone received the glory for those three thousand conversions.

I well remember one Sunday morning just before I was to preach at the eleven o'clock service. I had an argument with my wife, Louise. I should never have done it, but I stormed out, slamming the door in her face. Before I knew it, I was bowing my head on the upper platform at Westminster Chapel before several hundred people. I don't know what they were thinking, but I know what *I* was thinking: "I should not be here. I have no right to be here. Lord, how on earth could You use me today? I am not fit to be in this pulpit." It was too late to send a note to Louise saying, "I'm sorry." There was no way to resolve the situation at that time. I could only ask God for mercy and try my best to forgive myself. I assumed I was about to deliver the biggest flop of a sermon in the history of Westminster Chapel. Never in my life had I felt so unworthy. But when I stood up to preach, I was not prepared for the help I got. God simply undergirded me and enabled me to preach as well as I ever had! When we are emptied of all self-righteousness and pride, we enable God to move in and through us.

PERSONAL REFLECTION

Is there some action in the past for which you have been unable to forgive yourself? Why do you cling so tightly to the past? Have the vines of self blame overtaken your life and become a thorny fixture? What do you think it would feel like if you totally let yourself off the hook as God already has?

_____

_____

_____

_____

_____

_____

_____

_____

_____

DAY 18

Why Is It Hard to Forgive Yourself?

W HAT CAUSES OUR inability to forgive ourselves? At the end of the day why don't we do it? Today we'll explore a few reasons it can be harder than we think to let ourselves off the hook.

Anger

We may be angry with ourselves. Look at the Old Testament story of Joseph. As a type of Christ, Joseph said to his brothers, "And now, do not be distressed and do not be angry with yourselves for selling me here, because it was to save lives that God sent me ahead of you" (Gen. 45:5). These brothers were beginning to get the message that Joseph had forgiven them. But Joseph knew they would struggle with forgiving themselves. One of the proofs that Joseph had totally forgiven them was that he didn't want them to be angry with themselves.

That is the way God forgives. He doesn't want us to be angry with ourselves for our sins. Jesus forgives us in the same exact manner in which Joseph forgave his brothers; just as Joseph did not want his brothers to be angry with themselves, so Jesus does not want us to be angry with ourselves.

Not forgiving ourselves is self-hatred; it is being angry

81

with ourselves. Joseph's brothers had hated themselves for twenty-two years for selling Joseph into slavery. They could not turn the clock back or take back what they had done. They could not get a second chance.

Jesus says to you and me, "Don't be angry with yourself." Peter was none the worse for his denial of Jesus. He felt ashamed, yes. But his pride and ego were diminished, and I suspect he was easier to live with after that!

I have known some hypocritical Christians who became even more self-righteous after falling into sin; they began to justify all they had done. The answer to self-righteousness is not found in an opportunity to sin. Don't be a fool. But what is true is this: God can take your sinful past and make it work together for your good—so brilliantly and beautifully that you will be tempted to say that that is the way it was supposed to be!

Some Christians who can't forgive themselves are, underneath it all, angry with themselves. But God can begin today to cause all that happened to fit into a pattern for good. Begin to forgive yourself. And don't feel guilty about doing so! God says, "Take your forgiveness and don't look back." God will take the wasted years and restore them to good before it is all over. It is just as God promised in the Book of Joel: "I will repay you for the years the locusts have eaten" (Joel 2:25).

Fear

In some cases it is fear more than anger that is a barrier to our forgiving ourselves. Regret over the past leads to guilt, and guilt can lead to fear—the fear of missing "what might have been" or the fear that what has happened cannot possibly turn out for good.

Fear, then, is one of the main reasons we do not forgive ourselves. He or she who fears has not been made perfect in love, and "fear has to do with punishment" (1 John 4:18). But Paul tells us, "The Spirit you received does not make you slaves, so that you live in fear again; rather, the Spirit you received brought about your adoption to sonship. And by him we cry, '*Abba*, Father'" (Rom. 8:15, emphasis added). Paul said to Timothy, "For the Spirit God gave us does not make us timid, but gives us power, love and self-discipline" (2 Tim. 1:7).

Recognizing that fear—and punishing ourselves for our mistakes—displeases God should result in an ever-increasing sadness for this self-loathing spirit. We are required to walk away from our past folly. And when we are tempted to look back, we must obey that sign, "No trespassing allowed."

God speaks those words to us. Let the past be the past at last. Forgive yourself as well as those who have damaged you.

Pride, self-righteousness, and self-pity

At the end of the day our unforgiveness of ourselves may be traceable to pride. That is what is ultimately at work when we compete with the blood of Christ. We, in our arrogance and self-righteousness, cannot bear the Lord doing everything for us so graciously, so we think we must help Him out a bit. It is an abominable way to think. Our pride must be eclipsed by humility; we must let God be God and the blood of Christ do what it in fact did: remove our guilt and satisfy God's sense of justice.

Just as fear and pride are like identical twins, so are self-righteousness and self-pity. We feel sorry for ourselves and show it by not forgiving ourselves. That is why pseudoguilt can develop into very real and heinous guilt before God. It is false guilt since God says, "You're not guilty." We make it into real guilt when we in effect reply, "Yes I am."

The bottom line is this: not forgiving ourselves is wrong and dishonoring to God.

At this point you may be saying, "I agree. I know not forgiving myself is wrong. I just can't help it." What can be done to help you forgive yourself if you truly want to?

PERSONAL REFLECTION

Is there any choice you have made in your life that makes you instantly angry at yourself when you think about it? Pray about it and ask God what to do with this anger.

_____

_____

_____

_____

Are you generally an angry person? What positive purpose does anger serve? Does God see anger that way? How can you mature in this area?

_____

_____

_____

_____

Guilt vs. Grace

IF WE FEEL guilty, blame ourselves, and find that we cannot function normally—even though we have confessed our sins to God—it indicates that we haven't yet totally forgiven ourselves. It means that we are still hanging on to guilt that God has washed away; we are refusing to enjoy what God has freely given us. First John 1:9 either is true, or it isn't: "If we confess our sins, he is faithful and just and will forgive us our sins and purify us from all unrighteousness." If we have confessed our sins, we must take this promise with both hands and forgive ourselves—which is precisely what God wants us to do.

The person who hasn't forgiven himself is an unhappy person—and is usually unable to forgive others. Thus, my not forgiving myself will often backfire, and I will struggle to forgive others. Or my not forgiving others may result in a sense of shame that causes unforgiveness of myself. The irony is the degree to which we forgive others will often be the degree to which we forgive ourselves; the degree to which we set ourselves free will often be the degree to which we forgive others.

It is like the age-old question "Which comes first, the chicken or the egg?" It is sometimes almost impossible to say which comes first, forgiving others so you will be able to forgive yourself, or forgiving yourself so you will be able to forgive others. But it is not *total* forgiveness until both are equally true.

True guilt and pseudoguilt

There are two kinds of guilt most of us will struggle with: true guilt (a result of our sin against God) and pseudoguilt (when there is no sin in our lives). When we have sinned—as Joseph's brothers did and as Peter and the disciples did—we must confess it to God (1 John 1:9). The blood of Jesus takes care of true guilt by doing two basic things:

- It washes away our sin—as though it never existed.

- It perfectly satisfies God's eternal justice.

God is looking only to His Son's precious blood for satisfaction. Any chastening or discipline that comes from our Father is not adding to Jesus' blood. He is not getting even with us; He "got even" at the cross. The Greek word that translates as "chastening" or "discipline" in Hebrews 12:6 means enforced learning. When God teaches us a lesson, He makes sure we learn it! Whereas discipline is necessary because we are sinners, it does not follow that God is looking for more satisfaction for His just nature. Sin that has been confessed to God is totally forgiven by Him, and any guilt we feel after that is pseudoguilt.

There are also two kinds of this false guilt:

- When sin was never involved in the first place

- When sin has been forgiven

Pseudoguilt—though it is false—is also very real; that is, we feel keenly guilty. But it is called pseudoguilt because when it is thought through, there is *no good reason* for feeling guilty.

Take, for example, a person who is driving a car when a child runs out into the street at the last second and is struck down. The guilt can be overwhelming, but there was no sin. It doesn't need to be confessed to God.

Another example of false guilt is missing out on an opportunity. I have a friend in Florida who had a chance to buy a property many years ago for $5,000. He turned down the offer. Today that property is worth over $1 million. He feels guilty that he didn't use his money more wisely, but this is not true guilt.

The list of ways pseudoguilt can adversely affect our lives is endless. We can become weighed down over something that in actuality had nothing to do with us: not speaking to a person when you didn't even see him or her, not answering a letter you never received, and so on. These are not necessarily sins, but they can make us feel guilty.

The other kind of pseudoguilt is when you have confessed your sins—you may have even repented deeply—but you don't feel forgiven. Once you have acknowledged your sin, you should accept your forgiveness and leave the rest in God's hands.

Not forgiving ourselves is a subtle way of competing with Christ's atonement. God has already punished Jesus for what we did. (See 2 Corinthians 5:17.) When we don't accept our own forgiveness, we are punishing ourselves. Instead of accepting Jesus' sacrifice, I want to punish myself for my failures. This competes with Christ's finest hour.

Understanding guilt

The ability to forgive ourselves comes partly from understanding guilt. Guilt is, at heart, a feeling that one is to blame. For example, when you blame others, you have kept a record of their wrongs. But when you blame yourself, you have kept a record of your own wrongs. The Holy Spirit shows us our sin; the initial work of the Spirit according to John 16:8 is that He convicts of sin. When Isaiah saw the glory of the Lord, he was convicted of his sin (Isa. 6:1–5). When we walk in the light, we know the blood cleanses us of sin, but walking in the light also reveals sin in us that we may not have seen before (1 John 1:7–8).

But the sense of guilt God instigates is temporary.

> For his anger lasts only a moment, but his favor
> lasts a lifetime; weeping may stay for the night, but
> rejoicing comes in the morning.
>
> —PSALM 30:5

God uses guilt only to get our attention. When we say, "I'm sorry," and mean it, that's enough for God. He doesn't beat us black and blue and require us to go on a thirty-day fast to supplement Christ's atonement. He convicts us of sin to get our attention, but having done that, He wants us to move forward.

Understanding grace

The ability to forgive ourselves therefore extends from an understanding of grace. Grace is undeserved favor. Mercy is not getting what we do deserve (justice); grace is getting what we don't deserve (total forgiveness). Grace isn't grace if we have to be good enough for it to apply to us.

Peter *knew* what he had done and knew he was forgiven. David *knew* what he had done and pleaded for God's mercy

(Ps. 51). Grace is accepting what we don't deserve. It may seem unfair when we have been so horrible. We have let God down; we have let others down.

But it *is* fair, says John: "If we confess our sins, he is faithful and just and will forgive us our sins and purify us from all unrighteousness" (1 John 1:9). The blood of Jesus did a wonderful job. God is not looking for further satisfaction. We forgive ourselves to the degree we really do believe that!

All accusations regarding confessed sin come from the devil. When you know you have applied 1 John 1:9 but you still sense an accusing voice over that past failure, mark it down. That voice did not come from your heavenly Father. It did not come from Jesus. It did not come from the Holy Spirit. It came from your enemy, the devil, who works either as a roaring lion to scare or as an angel of light to deceive— or both (1 Pet. 5:8; 2 Cor. 11:14). Never forget, perfect love drives out fear (1 John 4:18).

PERSONAL REFLECTION

What issues haunt you with pseudoguilt? Pray and ask God to allow you to tell the difference between real guilt and pseudoguilt and that He will help you escape the haunting shadow of the latter.

_____

_____

_____

_____

_____

_____

_____

_____

_____

Make a mental list of the things for which you need to forgive yourself. Consider each one, and consciously let go of
your right to feel guilty about it or hold a grudge against
yourself. Over the next few days let that feeling grow into
something durable and lasting.

_____

_____

_____

_____

_____

_____

_____

_____

Four Things People Hold Against God

ALTHOUGH YOU MIGHT not see it yet as we cross the halfway point in our journey to total forgiveness, bitterness is ultimately traceable to a resentment of God. This may be an unconscious anger. Some of you might be horrified at the thought that you could be harboring bitterness toward God. But many repress this; such knowledge is too painful to admit.

Why do you feel this way? Because deep in your heart you believe that He is the one who allowed bad things to happen in your life. In a sense, you feel you have been betrayed by God. Since He is all-powerful and all-knowing, couldn't He have prevented tragedies and offenses from happening? He has allowed you to suffer when you didn't do anything, or so it seems, to warrant such ill treatment. What you ultimately believe is that God is to blame for your hurt.

My heart goes out to you if you wrestle with such feelings. I wrote the book *Totally Forgiving God* to encourage people who are struggling in their faith because they blame God for what has happened to them or someone they love. I use the example of Habakkuk, the Old Testament prophet who addressed the ancient problem of evil. Perhaps you can identify with one or more of his four basic complaints against God.

1. Unanswered prayer

In the book that bears his name, the ancient prophet's very first words are a prayer complaining that God does not listen: "How long, LORD, must I call for help, but you do not listen?" (Hab. 1:2).

The Hebrew word translated as "listen" is *shema*—a word that means to hear or to obey. If God hears in the Hebraic sense, it means He will *obey our request*. In other words, if He hears us, He will answer us. Habakkuk shows that God can simply *choose not to hear us*.

It is an eternal principle that any request prayed in the will of God will be answered. "This is the confidence we have in approaching God: that if we ask anything according to his will, he hears us" (1 John 5:14). So had Habakkuk not been praying in the will of God? After all, sometimes God's refusal to listen is owing to our willful disobedience. Had Habakkuk been disobedient? No. Habakkuk was interceding for Israel, God's people, and was no doubt caught in the cross fire between their disobedience and God venting His anger on them. Habakkuk's comment "You do not listen" referred to the way God seemed to be hiding His face from His people.

A natural response toward God when He does not answer our request is often to accuse Him of being uncaring and directly responsible for our hurt. And yet God is always motivating us to pray and seek His face with the promise that He will respond. We might read the words of such promises and pray for a good while, but when God doesn't answer in what we judge to be a reasonable length of time, we may feel let down or sometimes betrayed. For some the conclusion follows: "He must not be there at all. Why should I believe Him when He invites me to call on Him but does not answer?"

That reasoning of course is from our subjective perspective—the way it seems from our point of view. Are we then to set God free from any responsibility for not answering our prayers, and should we totally forgive Him? Yes.

2. God looking the other way during violence

Habakkuk's second complaint is that God does not see what is happening. "[I] cry out to you, 'Violence!' but you do not save?" (Hab. 1:2). This seems from our subjective perspective to be the consummate example of God betraying us. When I am seeking God's face and am right in the middle of violence, murder, rape, war, or torture, and God seems to turn His head away and look in another direction, what am I to believe? Why should I believe He is there? Why should I believe He cares? Why did this happen? Does this make sense? Those are the most natural questions in the world.

There are countless illustrations of people suffering violence even when they are attempting to do the will of God—missionaries in various parts of the world who are tortured, young Christians who rededicate their lives to Christ who are murdered, or restored backsliders who come back to the Lord who suddenly experience financial reverse or fatal illness. Instead of God rewarding them, the thanks some get are to suffer the most shameful kind of violence. I have counseled people sobbing their hearts out who were raped on their way to church, mugged on their way to a prayer meeting, or accosted during a time they were renewing their commitment to God. Who can explain why God would allow a violent man to interrupt a church service and start gunning down people right, left, and center? Or when He lets evil people commit acts of terrorism because of religious beliefs. Is there a perfectly right reason that God allows these things?

From our perspective, they make no sense. And yet are we to let God off the hook for all this? Yes.

3. Having to endure injustice

Habakkuk's third complaint was that God does not care. "Why do you make me look at injustice?" (Hab. 1:3). One of the most painful things many have to face is seeing injustice carried out in the courts—like someone getting away with murder.

With our modern-day access to media news twenty-four hours a day, the whole nation can become embroiled in the drama of court cases. One side or the other becomes indignant over the verdict when they feel that evil has won the day. This is to say nothing of the vast number of crimes— rape, murder, theft, torture, lying—that never get reported in newspapers or on television. Most cases never get enough profile in the media for people to take notice. When judges are bribed or juries are prejudiced, what are the innocent to do? Whereas some world leaders such as Adolf Hitler and dictators such as Saddam Hussein are found out, most are not. Think of the people who suffer at their hands. When we read of the account of six million Jews in the Holocaust or of black people being slaughtered during the apartheid days in South Africa, we ask, "Where was God in all this?" Are we to clear God's name in the light of this? Yes.

4. God's tolerance of evil

Habakkuk's fourth complaint was that God knowingly permits evil to thrive. "Why do you tolerate wrongdoing?" (Hab. 1:3). It is perhaps surprising that this question does not come up in the Bible more than it does. God is not offended by it. He is not threatened by it. And yet there are times when we are driven to our knees with tears and agony to ask why. There are awful things going on all over the world—famine, racial injustice, greed, corruption, war, unspeakable pain, theft, incurable diseases, and natural disasters such as hurricanes, earthquakes, and tsunamis. So we ask why.

What I myself have personally experienced in the way of disappointment in my lifetime is virtually nothing compared with what is existent all over the world. And yet I still ask a question that I asked for weeks and months after my mother's death in 1953 (she was only forty-three): Why? In those days someone gave me a recording of a song sung by a Southern gospel quartet called "We'll Talk It Over," which I listened to for hours and hours in the ensuing weeks. The words assured me that in time I would be able to ask God the reasons and He would give me answers.

PERSONAL REFLECTION

If a child asked you to explain the presence of evil in the world, what would you say?

_____

_____

_____

_____

_____

_____

_____

_____

_____

_____

Are you, or have you ever been, angry with God?

_____

_____

_____

_____

_____

_____

_____

_____

DAY 21

Five Steps to Forgiving God

YESTERDAY WE NAVIGATED some questions that arise when God doesn't make sense to us—questions such as "Why does God allow evil and suffering to continue when He has the power to stop it?" Only a fool would claim to know the full answer to such a question, but there is a partial answer: He does so in order that we may believe. There would be no need for faith if we knew the answer concerning the origin of evil and the reason for suffering. I only know that it is what makes faith possible.

I know something else as well.

> All things work together for good to them that love God, to them who are the called according to his purpose.
>
> —ROMANS 8:28, KJV

God does turn evil into blessing. He causes things to work together for good. God did not send His Son into the world to explain evil but rather to save us from it and to exemplify a life of suffering. Jesus, who was and is the God-man, suffered as no one else has or ever will. One day God will clear His own name from the charge of being unjust, but in the

97

meantime we need to trust Him and take Him at His word that He is just and merciful.

Overcoming hurts through total forgiveness is one of the most difficult things in the world to do. It is arguably the most major challenge one can accept in this life. I therefore put the following suggestions *not* as easy steps but rather as things for you to consider as a way forward in forgiving God, if you have not done so.

1. **Be totally honest with God and tell Him your complaint.** When you talk to God, be vulnerable, transparent, and totally honest with Him. Take the mask off. He sees right through you anyway! Don't pretend; don't try to impress Him. Tell Him your anger, your hurts, and your feeling of bewilderment. The more honest you are, the more intimate your relationship with Him will become. After all, why do you think He let you go through that trial in the first place? It was partly to get your attention. He likes your company. He wants a close relationship with you. The bottom line: it is all because He loves you so much.

2. **Make a list of things you are truly thankful for.** When you have been dealt a most severe blow, it is easy to forget the good things you have in life. With effort you can think of some things. The list will grow as you think harder. I strongly recommend you take time to reflect. Go back over your life. Write down every single thing you are happy about. Did you ever think to say thank you to the Lord for these things?

When you do this earnestly and thoughtfully, you will be amazed how long the list becomes.

3. **Fight self-pity and a feeling of entitlement with all your heart.** We come from our mothers' wombs with a feeling that God owes us something. It is symptomatic of the sin we inherited from the fall of our first parents in the Garden of Eden that we feel like this. We come into the world not only speaking lies but also feeling that God owes us certain things—explanations, income, comfort, and so on. In reality it is of God's mercy that we are not consumed (Lam. 3:22). If you will just pause and think, you will be amazed how much you have to be thankful for. My advice to you: tell God how thankful you are. He notices it when we don't thank Him. Make it a habit to tell Him of the things you are thankful for. Name them one by one.

4. **Choose to believe that God has a purpose in what He has permitted—and thank Him for it.** You may not be convinced yet that He has a purpose in what He has allowed. Don't worry. The worst suffering is the hardest to understand at first. The most natural reaction in the world is to panic and complain. But one day you will see that God was up to something wonderful. The God of the Bible is a God of purpose. He does nothing accidentally, and all accidents are under His all-seeing eye. The reason that all things work together for good to them that love God is because of God's purpose, plan, and

intention (Rom. 8:28). God does everything He does according to His sovereign plan; He works everything according to the purpose of His will (Eph. 1:11). What He said to others centuries ago He says now to you: "'For I know the plans I have for you,' declares the LORD, 'plans to prosper you and not to harm you, plans to give you hope and a future'" (Jer. 29:11).

5. **Be patient and willing to wait for things to become clear to you.** Perhaps one of the hardest things to do is to simply wait. What exactly are you to be waiting for? First, for the dust to settle and for things to become clearer to you. This may take time. It could take a long time. It might not even happen in the present life. There are some things I don't really expect to be cleared up for me in this life. Vindication does not always take place on this earth. We all have to wait for some things to be clear in heaven. Vindication for some will take place in heaven. Take heart. The things that have happened to you were not unseen by God. He loves justice and will vindicate you. Sometimes He does it in the present life; sometimes He waits. But I make you a promise: the longer He waits, the sweeter the vindication will be. I guarantee it. "Therefore judge nothing before the appointed time; wait till the Lord comes. He will bring to light what is hidden in darkness and will expose the motives of the heart. At that time each will receive his praise from God" (1 Cor. 4:5). That, dear reader, is worth waiting for.

As for all the unhappy things He has allowed to happen to me, I affirm His justice. He is God. He knows exactly what He is doing—and why. For all of us who struggle with God's right to allow evil to exist in the world, there still must be a genuine forgiveness on our part, for any bitterness toward God grieves the Holy Spirit. We therefore must forgive Him—though He is not guilty—for allowing evil to touch our lives.

If we will patiently wait for God's purposes to be fulfilled, at the end of the day—this is a guarantee—we will say that He has done all things well, even in what He permitted. He was never guilty in the first place, but because He sometimes appears to us to have been unfair, we must relinquish our bitterness and wholly forgive Him before we can move on with our lives.

PERSONAL REFLECTION

If you struggle with bitterness against God, write an honest, gut-level prayer asking Him to help you with your struggle.

_____

_____

_____

_____

_____

How to Know You Have Forgiven God

WE MUST BE careful how we talk about God, who allowed bad things to happen to us—although I completely understand when people say, "God must not love me because so many negative things have happened." Or some ask, "What have I done wrong that these things have happened to me?" You may recall that Job's so-called friends were convinced he had done something terrible, or God would not have let bad things happen to him. You may also recall that *they were completely wrong*.

Once you have truly and totally let God off the hook for what He allowed in your life, you should not keep saying that God must not love you or blame yourself because certain things have happened to you. The danger is that one can become bitter. Giving in to bitter feelings will not cause the bitterness to go away. Like looking at pornography, the more one indulges in it, the more one needs still more of it. In much the same way, venting one's bitterness or self-pity only causes you to get stirred up all the more. When we have been angry with God—but have forgiven Him—the first step is to guard our lips when we talk about God.

Tell God that you love Him. This may be the hardest thing you have ever had to do in your life. "But perfect love casts out fear" (1 John 4:18, NKJV), and when you perceive He wants to hear it from you, just maybe you will tell Him that you love Him.

With love, as with forgiveness, sometimes we must begin with *doing* rather than *feeling*. But whether your words spring from genuine affection or not, as soon as you are able to do so, tell God that you love Him. He wants to hear it from you. Perhaps tomorrow it will be easier than today. Keep it up. God is not offended that you are struggling in this area. He knows what we are like inside and out.

Set God free by overcoming self-pity. Most of us cannot forgive very easily until the people who hurt us are sorry for what they did. It takes minimal grace to forgive a person if he or she is sorry; it takes maximum grace to forgive when the person is not the slightest bit repentant. Jesus should be our model; He prayed for those who crucified Him when these men were not the slightest bit sorry for what they did. "Father, forgive them, for they do not know what they are doing" (Luke 23:34). We, however, naturally want to see people being sorry for what they did to us. This is partly because we are feeling sorry for ourselves that we had to be put through what they did to us. It is our self-pity that is a driving force in wanting our enemies to feel sorry; we want them to feel pity toward us!

But self-pity gets us nowhere with God. Absolutely nowhere. As James put it, our wrath "worketh not the righteousness of God" (James 1:20, KJV). We may wish that our sulking and hurt might move God to feel pity for us. I'm sorry, but it doesn't work that way. As long as we are feeling sorry for ourselves and are hoping this will make God sorry for what He allowed in our lives, we can dream on! I wish it weren't so! But self-pity does not make God say, "I'm so sorry for allowing you to go through this," as if He owes us an apology. Self-pity is our unsubtle attempt to manipulate God. He doesn't fall for it. Set God totally free by refusing to make Him feel He has wronged you. Don't go there. Don't even think it!

Affirm the greater purpose God had in mind when He allowed you to suffer. As I've said, total forgiveness is not easy. You may need time to come to terms with God and His allowing what He did in letting you suffer so much. It is only a matter of time when you will see that God permitted what He did in your life because He had a purpose in it. It was not for nothing. It was not an accident. You have not been randomly thrown into your existence without meaning. God created you and is the ruler over all. A leaf falls from a tree by His hand. He feeds the sparrows. He clothes the earth with beauty. He knows how many hairs are on your head. Whatever has happened to you was not when He had His head turned. He was looking straight at you.

Totally forgiving God is what you will have to do for the rest of your life. I call it a life sentence. As a physician may give a patient a tablet telling him or her, "You will have to take this for the rest of your life," so it is with total forgiveness.

It is not enough to say once to God: "I let You off the hook; I do forgive You." You may have to do it again tomorrow. Next week. Next year. Ten years from now. It is a life commitment, a life sentence; to show you meant it, you do it on and on and on. The devil will do all he can to remind you of the evil things done to you and try to make you bitter toward God all over again. Don't listen to him. In a few more days we'll review the three Rs of spiritual warfare: recognize, refuse, and resist. Do not be surprised that your enemy the devil will remind you of the evil that came upon you to make you angry with God. Recognize Satan, refuse to listen to him, and resist him—and he will flee from you.

Bless the Lord for all He has done in your life. Jesus told us to bless our enemies (Luke 6:27–28). You may recall that when Job was first hit by horrible suffering, he graciously said, "The LORD gave and the LORD has taken away; may the name of the LORD be praised" (Job 1:21). If only Job had maintained that position!

Perhaps you felt God was like an enemy when He first allowed you to go through unthinkable disappointment and suffering—when He could have so easily stopped it. But He didn't. He let you go through deep, deep hurt. But given sufficient time you saw that He was with you after all. I am saying to you: bless the Lord, who seemed like your enemy. The sooner you can praise the Lord—as if like blessing your enemy—the better. The day will come that it won't be an effort to do it. It will be easier and easier and easier.

PERSONAL REFLECTION

Is it possible to totally forgive? I declare, yes! Write some evidences of total forgiveness that you have encountered on this road of forgiveness. We'll explore more evidences of total forgiveness in the next section.

_____

_____

_____

_____

Do You Know if You've Forgiven—Totally?

DAY 23

Joseph's Example of Total Forgiveness

OVER THE YEARS I've been asked many times, "How can I know whether I have truly forgiven someone?" I have discovered that the account of Joseph forgiving his brothers in Genesis 45 provides a heart-searching frame of reference in answer to this question.

Twenty-two years earlier Joseph's brothers had conspired to kill him because they were jealous of the attention he got from their father. As Jacob's favorite child Joseph strutted around in a richly ornamented robe of many colors. In addition, Joseph dreamed that his eleven brothers would one day come begging to him, and he showed no sensitivity or humility at all in telling them. (See Genesis 37:6–9.)

God's hand was on Joseph's life, but because this young man needed to learn temperance, God allowed Joseph's brothers to deal with him ruthlessly. Instead of killing him, they decided on plan B—selling him as a slave to the Ishmaelites. This they did, never expecting to see him again.

In order to explain Joseph's sudden absence to their father, the brothers concocted a clever cover-up. They dipped Joseph's robe in some goat's blood and took it to Jacob. They deceived him, saying, "We found this. Examine it to see whether it is your son's robe" (Gen. 37:32). The plan worked.

Even though the situation looked bleak, God was with Joseph. He began to work in the house of Potiphar, the Egyptian officer to whom the Ishmaelites had sold him. He was such a valuable employee that he was put in charge of the entire household. But Potiphar's wife began to flirt with him. "Come to bed with me!" she pleaded, but he refused.

After being rejected repeatedly, she decided to accuse Joseph of rape. Potiphar believed his wife and had Joseph put in prison. Joseph was punished for doing the right thing! This was the beginning of a period of preparation for Joseph. He didn't realize it at the time, but God had great plans for him.

Joseph had much to be bitter about and many "offenders" to forgive: his brothers, who sold him into slavery; Potiphar's wife, who lied; and God, who let it all happen.

After some time passed, Joseph had company in prison—Pharaoh's cupbearer and baker. While there each of them had a dream that Joseph offered to interpret. He predicted that the baker would be hanged in three days but that the cupbearer would get his job back in the same span of time. Both of those events took place just as Joseph predicted. So far, so good.

But a temptation too great—so it seemed—was handed to Joseph on a silver platter. He had barely finished telling the cupbearer that he would be restored to Pharaoh's favor when Joseph got too involved in his prophetic word.

> But when all goes well with you, remember me and show me kindness; mention me to Pharaoh and get me out of this prison. I was forcibly carried off from the land of the Hebrews, and even here I have done nothing to deserve being put in a dungeon.
> —Genesis 40:14–15

Most of us would have done the same thing. But God had special plans for Joseph, and in order for his testimony to be validated later, there could be no promotion that could be explained in terms of what a human being could do. In other words, God wanted Joseph out of prison as much as Joseph wanted to get out. But if the cupbearer simply put in a good word for Joseph—and he was sprung from prison because of it—it would have fallen far short of God's supreme plan. Delays can actually be part of God's purpose; seemingly unanswered prayer can be as much a part of God's will as answered prayer.

The truth is Joseph needed to be delivered from bitterness and self-pity. First Corinthians 13:5, the same verse that says love "keeps no record of wrongs," also says that love "is not self-seeking." If we are walking in love, we will not play the manipulator when it comes to promoting ourselves; we will let God promote us in His timing. Joseph was full of self-pity. He says so: "I have done nothing to deserve being put in a dungeon" (Gen. 40:15). Self-pity and self-righteousness—twin sins that complement each other—are eclipsed when we begin to forgive totally and keep no record of wrongs. At that point in time Joseph had not yet forgiven his brothers, Potiphar's wife, or God.

Joseph had not forgotten his dreams. He knew that one day—for one reason or another—his brothers would bow down before him. And eventually they did. But when it finally happened, Joseph was a changed man. There was no bitterness. There were no grudges. None. Something had happened to him during those final two years in prison. How do I know that? Look at him; listen to him! His attitude had completely changed. He had totally and wonderfully forgiven them all. Before his heart was changed, he probably fantasized about the day they would come begging him for forgiveness; he probably longed to see the fulfillment of his dreams, to say "Gotcha!" to his brothers, and then to throw the book at them. Instead, when the time came, he lovingly welcomed them and forgave them with tears.

What caused such a dramatic change? Two years after Joseph had interpreted the dreams of the baker and the cupbearer, Pharaoh himself had a dream—two dreams in fact—and none of his magicians and astrologers could figure them out. The cupbearer overheard the commotion and remembered how Joseph had interpreted his dream so accurately. He stepped forward and recommended Joseph to Pharaoh. Suddenly Joseph found himself before the ruler of Egypt, and he alone was able to interpret the dreams: there would be seven years of plenty followed by seven years of famine in the land. Joseph also offered his advice: Pharaoh should store up food during the first seven years so that there would be a surplus available during the seven years of lack—not only for Egypt but also for the surrounding countries that would come to Egypt begging for food.

Pharaoh was so impressed with this wise advice that he made Joseph the prime minister of Egypt right on the spot! God did it all. He had used the cupbearer, yes, but not because of Joseph's manipulation.

Then, during the time of famine, who do you suppose came to Egypt begging for food? Joseph's brothers. He recognized them instantly, though they didn't know who he was—twenty-two years older and wearing official Egyptian garb, not to mention speaking Egyptian through an interpreter. The moment finally came when Joseph revealed himself. It was the moment he dreamed of. But instead of punishing them, which he had the power to do, he wept. Filled with love, he demonstrated total forgiveness.

In the next several days we'll explore how Joseph's example of total forgiveness applies to our lives.

PERSONAL REFLECTION

Recall a time in your life when you went through a period of "punishment" and discipline at God's hand. How did you get through this time?

_____

_____

_____

_____

_____

Have you been through times of preparation in your life? What was your attitude during these times? How did your attitude affect the length of time? When did you realize that the attitude of your heart was not right with God?

_____

_____

_____

_____

_____

You've Forgiven When You Don't Need to Talk About It

To ensure privacy, Joseph cried out, "Have everyone leave my presence!" (Gen. 45:1). He waited to reveal his identity until there was no one in the room except his brothers. Even the interpreter, who had no idea Joseph could speak Hebrew, was, to his surprise, told to leave.

But why? Why did Joseph make everyone else leave? Because he did not want a single person in Egypt to know what his brothers had done to him twenty-two years before. He had a plan—namely, to persuade them to bring their father, Jacob, to Egypt. He wanted his entire family there with him. No one in Egypt needed to know what they had done.

Joseph was a hero in Egypt. The people were in awe of him. By interpreting Pharaoh's dreams, he had saved the nation. He knew that if the word leaked out that his brothers had actually kidnapped him and sold him to Ishmaelites, the Egyptians would hate his brothers. Instead, Joseph wanted them to be heroes in Egypt as he was, and the only way to cause that to happen was to ensure that absolutely nobody in Egypt would ever discover their wickedness. So he did not allow anyone to eavesdrop on the historic conversation in Genesis 45 as he revealed his identity to his startled, frightened brothers. Not only did Joseph not let anybody know what they had done; he ensured that no one *could* know. That is one of the proofs that one has totally forgiven.

This is precisely how you and I are forgiven: "As far as the east is from the west, so far has he removed our transgressions from us" (Ps. 103:12). Our sins are "wiped out" (Acts 3:19). It is as though our sins don't exist anymore—they are gone, gone, gone, gone! Insofar as our standing and security with God are concerned, they will never be held against us. Back in the hills of Kentucky we used to sing a chorus about our sins being buried in God's sea of forgetfulness. This is based on Micah 7:19: "You will again have compassion on us; you will tread our sins underfoot and hurl all our iniquities into the depths of the sea."

God will not reveal what He knows. Picture, if you will, a giant screen such as the ones many churches use for projecting the words to worship songs. Imagine your sins listed on that screen for people to see. You would look at the list and be forced to admit, "Yes—that's true. But I thought I was forgiven and that nobody would know!" Imagine the sense of betrayal you would feel if God disclosed to everyone else what He knows about you!

There are a lot of things God knows about me that I wouldn't want anyone else to know. He has enough on me to bury me! But you will never know any of it because God won't tell.

So why do we tell on other people? If for therapeutic reasons we tell one other person, who will never repeat it, that is understandable. But the real reason we usually tell is to *punish*. And one weapon at our disposal to accomplish this is our tongue. We tell everyone else what we know in order to make our offender look bad! If we can hurt his or her credibility or reputation in return for hurting us, "Good!" we say. "It serves them right." We blab to everyone we can find what was done to us as a way of getting even.

Joseph is sometimes referred to as a type of Christ—a person in the Old Testament who, long before Jesus came along, displayed characteristics of Jesus Himself. And despite his imperfections Joseph was indeed a type of Christ in many ways. His ability to forgive his brothers as he did foreshadowed Jesus' actions toward His disciples. Scared to death and ashamed over the way they had deserted Jesus when He was arrested, they were huddled behind closed doors when the resurrected Jesus turned up unexpectedly and declared, "Peace be with you!" (John 20:21). The disciples were totally forgiven—and they knew it.

We all have skeletons in our closets. Some are known to others; many are unknown. It is comforting to know that God freely and totally forgives all our sins and will never tell what He knows. That is the way Joseph forgave. And that is why we are urged, "Be kind and compassionate to one another, forgiving each other, just as in Christ God forgave you" (Eph. 4:32).

When We Should Speak of the Grievance

"But what about the rapist?" you may ask. "Or the child abuser? Shouldn't the authorities be told?"

Can a person totally forgive and yet at the same time be the one who reports a crime? Absolutely. Total forgiveness does not mean closing our eyes to those who will continue to harm others. The apostle Paul ordered that the incestuous man in Corinth be put out of the church lest the entire church become corrupted. (See 1 Corinthians 5:5.) The rapist should be apprehended. The child abuser should be reported to the police, or he will continue to cause damage.

The types of offenses I primarily deal with in *Total Forgiveness* and related books such as this one do not pertain to crimes that have been committed or scandalous sins that bedevil the church. Most of us do not encounter those situations on a day-to-day basis. Instead, I address the small offenses that occur in daily life—the ones most Christians struggle to overcome, the ones that tempt us to harbor grudges and dream of revenge.

There is admittedly a very thin line between the desire to see a rapist or child abuser punished because the person is a danger to society and wanting the person put in prison because he or she has hurt us or someone we love. The actual victim of the abuse is in a particular quandary. When we are personally offended, we usually disqualify ourselves from being the one to remove the speck from another's eye. (See Matthew 7:5.) But a person who has been raped must be a witness in a courtroom while simultaneously forgiving the offender. This is not easy!

There is also often a need to talk to someone about how you have been hurt, and this can be therapeutic if it is done with the right heart attitude. If you must share with someone else—because you can't contain the pain—tell only one person, and carefully choose someone who won't repeat it to those it does not concern.

Examine your motives and be sure you aren't doing it to punish anyone by making the person look bad. This isn't necessarily easy sometimes, but when our motive is to hurt another person by telling on that person, there is sin on our part. When that is the case, do not tell it at all or in part; keep it quiet.

PERSONAL REFLECTION

Has anyone "forgiven" you, then betrayed your trust with what he or she knew about you? What did it do to your reputation? Your emotional life? Your relationship with that person?

_____

_____

_____

Have you made the mistake of sharing secrets about people you had forgiven? When did you realize you were wrong, and what did you do about it?

_____

_____

_____

Do you find it difficult to stop talking about the offenses you have suffered? What can you do to improve immediately in this area?

_____

_____

_____

You've Forgiven When You Don't Want Them to Be Intimidated

JOSEPH REVEALED HIS identity to his brothers with tears and compassion. The last thing he wanted was for them to fear him. He had been aching to let them know who he was, but he was following a carefully thought-out strategy and wanted to be sure the plan would work. When he could "no longer control himself," he broke down and told them who he was. "And he wept so loudly that the Egyptians heard him, and Pharaoh's household heard about it" (Gen. 45:2).

Joseph's immediate concern was not only to reveal who he was to his brothers but also to learn the condition of his father.

> Joseph said to his brothers, "I am Joseph! Is my father still living?" But his brothers were not able to answer him, because they were terrified at his presence.
>
> —GENESIS 45:3

When we have not totally forgiven those who hurt us, it gives us a bit of pleasure to realize that they are afraid or intimidated. If someone who has hurt us—and knows it—freezes in anxiety when he or she sees us approaching, we may say to ourselves, "Good! They *should* be afraid of me!" But that only shows that there is still bitterness in our hearts. "Perfect love drives out fear, because fear has to do with punishment" (1 John 4:18). If people are afraid of us, we fancy they are getting a bit of punishment—which is what we want if we are not walking in forgiveness.

But this was not the pattern of Joseph's life. Knowing they were "terrified at his presence," he said to them, "Come close to me" (Gen. 45:4). Why did he direct them to do this? For two reasons: he did not want them to be afraid, and he longed to embrace every single one of them—which he later did.

Fear can cause us to do silly things. Our insecurity is what causes us to want people to stand in awe of us. We become pretentious; we try to keep other people from knowing who we really are and what we are really like. Sometimes I think the most attractive thing about Jesus as a man was His unpretentiousness. Jesus did not try to create an "aura of mystique"; even common people could relate to Him.

In terms of prestige and power, Joseph had ascended as high as one could. Had he so desired, he could have kept his brothers at a distance. He could have demanded that they praise him for his success; he could have made them fall at his feet in fear and reverence. He could have reminded them of his dreams and their disbelief. He could have even said one of the favorite phrases of human beings everywhere: "I told you so."

But no. That is not what Joseph did. "Come close to me," he said. He did not feel a cut above them. He had no desire for them to stand back and say, "Wow! Look at our brother Joseph." He wanted them to feel no fear in his presence. He wanted to be loved rather than admired.

Paul said, "The Spirit you received does not make you slaves, so that you live in fear again; rather, the Spirit you received brought about your adoption to sonship. And by him we cry, '*Abba*, Father'" (Rom. 8:15, emphasis added). The word Abba is a pure Aramaic word that is the equivalent of the word daddy. The witness of the Holy Spirit makes us feel loved and accepted. Once He has forgiven us, God does not want us to be afraid of Him. This should not mean that we develop a cheap familiarity with Him, much less lose a sense of His glory and might, but He wants us to experience His fatherly tenderness.

What Joseph wanted his brothers to feel is what Jesus wants us to feel about Himself and the Father. "Anyone who has seen me has seen the Father," Jesus said (John 14:9). If you had an abusive or absentee father, you may understandably have trouble relating to God as a Father. But there is no law that says we have to have perfect fathers before we can rightly relate to our heavenly Father. The perfect image for us to follow can be found in Jesus Christ—and it is also what Joseph was trying to convey to his brothers. Joseph did not require them to feel a trace of fear or show further how sorry they were before he forgave them; instead, he wanted them to love him and feel his love for them in return.

This is the kind of relationship that Jesus desires with us. He wants to put us at ease in His presence. When Jesus met with the eleven disciples in the Upper Room after His resurrection, there was no hint of rebuke for their desertion and betrayal before His crucifixion. Jesus never said, "How could you have abandoned Me like that?" Instead, He picked up where He left off before the whole ordeal began and said, "As the Father has sent me, I am sending you" (John 20:21).

"There is no fear in love" (1 John 4:18). Joseph did not want his brothers to be afraid, and when we have totally forgiven our offenders, we will not want them to be afraid either.

PERSONAL REFLECTION

Have you ever trembled in the presence of someone you wronged? Was he or she able to put you at ease?

_____

_____

_____

_____

_____

How do you make yourself accessible and real to people who wronged you?

_____

_____

_____

_____

_____

DAY 26

You've Forgiven When You Can
Set Them Free From Guilt

WHEN THE ELEVEN brothers had difficulty believing Joseph's revelation, he repeated it: "I am your brother Joseph, the one you sold into Egypt!" (Gen. 45:4). He had not forgotten what they had done, nor did he pretend that it hadn't happened; he was simply identifying himself to them.

Knowing exactly what they were thinking, he said, "And now, do not be distressed and do not be angry with yourselves for selling me here" (Gen. 45:5). He was not about to send them on a guilt trip; he knew that they felt guilty enough (Gen. 42:21).

Sometimes we say, in effect, "I forgive you for what you did, but I hope you feel bad about it." This shows we still want to see the person punished. It shows our own fear, which, I repeat, "has to do with punishment" (1 John 4:18). But when our fear is gone, the desire to see others punished goes with it.

We love to punish people by making them feel guilty. Those of us who are always sending people on guilt trips almost certainly have a big problem ourselves with a sense of guilt. Because we haven't sorted out our own guilt issues, we want to

123

make sure others wallow in the mire of guilty feelings with us. We point the finger partly because we haven't forgiven ourselves.

I sometimes think guilt is one of the most painful feelings in the world. My own greatest pain over the years has been guilt—and being reminded of my own failure, especially as a parent. If someone wanted to hurt me—to really and truly make me feel awful—all he or she would have to do is ask, "How much time did you spend with your kids in those critical years as they were growing up?" I am grateful that my children have totally forgiven me for my sins as a parent, but I still struggle with feelings of guilt for the mistakes that I made.

Joseph wanted to set his brothers free. He did not want them to blame or be angry with themselves; he wanted them to forgive themselves. Forgiveness is worthless to us emotionally if we can't forgive ourselves. And it certainly isn't *total* forgiveness unless we forgive ourselves as well as others.

God knows this. This is why He wants us to forgive ourselves as well as accept His promise that our past is under the blood of Christ. Joseph was trying to do what Jesus would do: make it easy for his brothers to forgive themselves.

To ease their minds, Joseph gave an explanation for his suffering: "It was to save lives that God sent me ahead of you" (Gen. 45:5). God does that with us as well; He wants to make it easy for us to forgive ourselves. That is partly why He gave us what is possibly Paul's most astonishing promise.

> And we know that all things work together for good
> to them that love God, to them who are the called
> according to his purpose.
>
> —Romans 8:28, kjv

God doesn't want us to continue to feel guilty, so He says, "Just wait and see. I will cause everything to work together for good to such an extent that you will be tempted to say that even the bad things that happened were good and right." Not that they were, of course, for the fact that all things work together for good doesn't mean necessarily that they were right at the time. But God has a way of making bad things *become* good.

This, then, is total forgiveness: not wanting our offenders to feel guilty or upset with themselves for what they did and showing them that there is a reason God let it happen.

PERSONAL REFLECTION

What was the most astonishing experience you have had of something good coming from bad circumstances?

_____

_____

_____

_____

_____

_____

_____

_____

Do you believe good can come from any bad event, or are some too awful? How does your view square with Romans 8:28?

_____

_____

_____

_____

_____

What circumstances are there in your life now that you want to turn from bad to good?

_____

_____

_____

_____

_____

_____

You've Forgiven When You Can Let Them Save Face

ALLOWING THOSE WHO have offended you to save face is carrying the principle of total forgiveness a step further. Joseph told his brothers something that is, without doubt, the most magnanimous, gracious, and emancipating statement he had made so far: "You didn't do this to me; God did."

> But God sent me ahead of you to preserve for you a remnant on earth and to save your lives by a great deliverance. So then, it was not you who sent me here, but God. He made me father to Pharaoh, lord of his entire household and ruler of all Egypt.
> —GENESIS 45:7–8

This is as good as it gets. When we can forgive like that, we're there. We have achieved total forgiveness.

Saving face. It is what God lets us do.

What exactly is *saving face*? Dale Carnegie uses this expression in his book *How to Win Friends and Influence People*. Although this is not specifically a Christian book, it is saturated with Christian principles and would do most Christians no harm to read. *Saving face* means preserving one's dignity and self-esteem. It is not only the refusal to let a person feel guilty; it is providing a rationale that enables what the person did to look good rather than bad. Or it may mean hiding a person's error from people so he or she can't be embarrassed.

You can make a friend for life by letting someone save face. I gather this is an Oriental expression, because for an Oriental the worst thing on earth is to lose face. Some have been known to commit suicide rather than lose face. But I have a suspicion that deep down we are all the same when it comes to losing face—none of us want it to happen.

God lets us save face by causing our past (however foolish) to work out for our good. If you read the genealogy of Jesus in Matthew 1, you might think that the sin of adultery between David and Bathsheba was part of the divine strategy all along. I doubt that is the case. David's sin of adultery—and the attempted cover-up involving the murder of Uriah—must rank as one of the worst crimes in the history of God's people. But Matthew 1:6 records these events as though what happened was supposed to have happened in just that way.

Can you imagine the looks on the faces of Joseph's brothers when he said to them, "So then it was not you who sent me here, but God" (Gen. 45:8)? Reuben may have said to Judah, "Did we hear him correctly? Did he say that we didn't do what we did, but God did it instead?" To have believed a statement like that would have meant an unimaginable burden of guilt rolled off these men. It would have been news too good to be true.

How could this be? According to Joseph, the answer was simple: God predestined that Abraham's descendants would live in Egypt. He simply sent Joseph ahead of the rest of his family. In other words, Joseph was literally saying, "Somebody had to go first, and I was chosen. God knew about the famine and that our family, the family of Israel, had to be preserved."

There is more. By saying what he did, Joseph was also admitting that if he had been in their shoes, he would have done what they did. He did not condemn them for what they did. He had reached an understanding of their actions.

For the one who totally forgives from the heart, there is little self-righteousness. Two reasons we are *able* to forgive are:

- We see what we ourselves have been forgiven of.

- We see what we are capable of.

When we are indignant over someone else's wickedness, there is the real possibility that either we are self-righteous or we have no objectivity about ourselves. When we truly see ourselves as we are, we will recognize that we are just as capable of committing any sin as anyone else. We are saved only by God's intervening grace.

This was no self-righteous man reaching out to his brothers. Joseph was not being condescending or patronizing, nor was he consciously performing some great feat. He was not thinking, "I will be admired for being so gracious to these unworthy, evil men." Quite the contrary; Joseph had already forgiven his brothers during those two years in the dungeon when God operated on his heart. He became a trophy of sovereign grace, an example of forgiveness for us to follow.

Letting his brothers save face, then, was not simply a polite gesture; Joseph was telling his brothers the truth. God *had* meant it for good; God *did* send Joseph to Egypt with a purpose in mind. Joseph was not one whit better than a single one of them, and he was not about to act like it. He simply felt grateful to see them again and grateful to God for everything that he had been brought through. The preparation, the false accusations, all the lies, pain, and suffering were worth it.

It is reminiscent of Jesus' words to His disciples: "A woman giving birth to a child has pain because her time has come; but when her baby is born she forgets the anguish because of her joy that a child is born into the world. So with you: Now is your time of grief, but I will see you again and you will rejoice, and no one will take away your joy" (John 16:21–22).

When we let people save face, we are doing what is right and just, not being merely magnanimous and gracious.

PERSONAL REFLECTION

When was the last time someone let you save face to escape monumental embarrassment? How did it make you feel toward that person? Grateful? Wary? Astonished?

_____

_____

_____

_____

_____

_____

_____

_____

_____

_____

What are the ways that you can help coworkers, family members, or friends save face as situations arise in daily life?

_____

_____

_____

_____

_____

_____

_____

_____

_____

DAY 28

You've Forgiven When You Can Protect Them From Their Greatest Fear

WHEN JOSEPH REVEALED his identity and expressed forgiveness, what do you suppose the eleven brothers were thinking? They were no doubt thrilled that their brother really and truly accepted them. The relief must have been sweet beyond words. But no sooner had they absorbed the good news than they experienced the greatest fear of all: they would have to return to Canaan and tell their father the truth of what they did.

You can be sure that they would rather have died than face their aged father with the truth behind that bloodstained coat of many colors that had been laid before him. For years their worst nightmare had been that their father would find out about their deception. Now they were faced with the prospect of returning to Canaan to persuade their father to move to Egypt, where his beloved Joseph was—would you believe—the prime minister. Jacob would certainly wonder how such a miracle was possible.

Joseph, knowing their guilt and dread, had already anticipated this problem and was a step ahead of his brothers. He knew that his forgiveness of what they had done was utterly

132

worthless to them if they had to tell the whole truth to their father.

This to me is one of the most moving scenes in this story. Joseph instructed his brothers to tell their father the truth—that he, Joseph, was alive and well and had become the prime minister of Egypt. Indeed, he told them exactly what to say and what *not* to say to Jacob. His direction was worded carefully, and it told their father all the truth that he needed to know. (See Genesis 45:9–13.)

Sin that is under the blood of our sovereign Redeemer does not need to be confessed to anyone but God. If you need to share your situation with one other person for therapeutic purposes, fine. But you should not involve an innocent person by unloading information on the person that he or she can easily live without. Instead, confess your sin to God.

> Against you, you only, have I sinned and done what
> is evil in your sight; so you are right in your verdict
> and justified when you judge.
>
> —Psalm 51:4

You may think the brothers should have confessed their sin to their father. Really? Wouldn't that have given Jacob an even greater problem—having to struggle with the regret of lost years with Joseph and with bitterness against his other sons?

Joseph was wise, loving, and fair. And it made his brothers respect him all the more.

When I consider the fact that our Lord Jesus Christ knows all about my sin but promises to keep what He has forgiven a carefully guarded secret, it increases my gratitude to Him.

Many of us have one single greatest fear. I know I do. I know what I would fear the most—were it to be told. But

God has no desire to hold our fears over our heads. I am indebted to my wonderful Savior, who forgives all my sins and will ensure that my greatest fears will never be realized.

God does not blackmail us. And when a person is guilty of blackmailing someone else, it gets God's attention. He won't stand for it. Holding another person in perpetual fear by threatening, "I'll tell on you," will quickly bring down the wrath of God. When I ponder the sins for which I have been forgiven, it is enough to shut my mouth for the rest of my life.

PERSONAL REFLECTION

How have you gone the extra mile and protected someone from his or her greatest fear?

_____

_____

_____

Think about your greatest fear, your ugliest secret. How does this fear affect you today? Pray and ask God to free you from it and give you rest from your past.

_____

_____

_____

You've Forgiven When You Can Make a Lifelong Commitment

MAKING A LIFELONG commitment to total forgiveness means that you keep on doing it—for as long as you live. It isn't enough to forgive today and then return to the offense tomorrow. I heard of a person whose wife said, "I thought you forgave me." He replied, "That was yesterday." Total forgiveness is a lifelong commitment, and you may need to practice it every single day of your life until you die. No one said it would be easy.

Seventeen years after reuniting with his long-lost son, Jacob died. Joseph's brothers suddenly panicked. They were terrified that Joseph's forgiveness would last only as long as their aged patriarch was still alive, that Joseph would at long last take revenge on them. We can understand their fears. Joseph's forgiveness was no ordinary thing; they had been incredibly blessed by his graciousness. But they feared it had come to an end: "When Joseph's brothers saw that their father was dead, they said, 'What if Joseph holds a grudge against us and pays us back for all the wrongs we did to him?'" (Gen. 50:15).

Because of their fear, they concocted a story.

> So they sent word to Joseph, saying, "Your father
> left these instructions before he died: 'This is what
> you are to say to Joseph: I ask you to forgive your
> brothers the sins and the wrongs they committed
> in treating you so badly.' Now please forgive the
> sins of the servants of the God of your father."
> —Genesis 50:16–17

If Jacob had really said this, he would not have just told Joseph's brothers; he would have told Joseph himself before he died. He would not have gone to his grave with a fear that Joseph would not forgive them. It was the brothers who were afraid.

When Joseph heard this message, he wept. He could not believe that his brothers doubted him. He could see that they lived in fear that one day he, the prime minister, would use his power to take vengeance on his brothers.

> But Joseph said to them, "Don't be afraid. Am I in
> the place of God? You intended to harm me, but
> God intended it for good to accomplish what is now
> being done, the saving of many lives. So then, don't
> be afraid. I will provide for you and your children."
> And he reassured them and spoke kindly to them.
> —Genesis 50:19–21

What Joseph had done seventeen years before still held good; he was prepared to care for his brothers indefinitely. "I forgave you then, and I forgive you now," he was saying to them. Joseph's change of heart was no passing thing. It was real. I have seen some people cave in and return to the offense after they extended their forgiveness to someone. But it is not total forgiveness unless it lasts—no matter how great the temptation is to turn back. I wonder if this is the "folly" that is referred to in Psalm 85:8: "I will listen to what God the LORD says; he promises peace to his people, his faithful servants—but let them not turn to folly."

I know that in my own life the temptation to return to bitterness can be very real. I concoct conversations in my head, imagining what I might say or recalling what had taken place, and I get churned up. The thought that no one will ever know or they are getting away with this agitates me. But if I take a step back and observe the situation from a distance, I can see the folly of such thinking. I have to keep on forgiving. Total forgiveness must go on and on and on. Some days will be harder than others.

I must never tell what I know, cause my offenders to feel fear, make them feel guilty, hope they will lose face, or reveal their most devastating secrets. And I must keep this up as long as I live.

If you are prepared to make a covenant to forgive—and to forgive totally—you must realize you will have to renew that covenant tomorrow. And it may be even harder to do tomorrow than it is today. It could even be harder next week or next year. But this is a lifetime commitment.

PERSONAL REFLECTION

Have you experienced ups and downs since embarking on this journey of forgiveness? What are the easy days of forgiveness like? What about the hard days?

_____

_____

_____

_____

_____

What thoughts haunt you in the "down" times when revenge and bitterness seem so attractive? Which scriptures have helped you in tough times when forgiveness seemed impossible?

_____

_____

_____

_____

_____

What benefits have you started to experience from your choice to forgive?

_____

_____

_____

_____

_____

DAY 30

You've Forgiven When You Can Pray for Them to Be Blessed

TOTAL FORGIVENESS INVOLVES an additional element: praying for God's blessings to rain on the lives of your offenders. "But I tell you, love your enemies and pray for those who persecute you" (Matt. 5:44). When you do this as Jesus intends it, you are being set free indeed.

To truly pray for the people who hurt you means to pray that they will be blessed, that God will show favor to rather than punish them, that they will prosper in every way. In other words, you pray that they will be dealt with as you want God to deal with you. You apply the Golden Rule as you pray. (See Matthew 7:12.) You don't pray, "God, deal with them." You don't pray, "Lord, get them for what they did to me." And neither is it enough to say, "Father, I commend them to You." That's a cop-out. You must pray that they receive total forgiveness, just as you want it for yourself.

Praying like this, to quote John Calvin, "is exceedingly difficult." St. John Chrysostom (c. 344–407) called it the "very highest summit of self-control."[1] And yet Job's suffering did not end until he prayed for those "friends" who had become his thorn in the flesh (Job 42:10). When we do this, we are

139

becoming more like our heavenly Father. (See Matthew 5:44–48.) That is true godliness, the very essence of Christlikeness.

To me the greatest inspiration to live in this manner is found in the life—and death—of Stephen. He is one of my heroes. When I read Acts 6:8–15 and consider the Holy Spirit's touch on his life, his enemies' inability to contradict his wisdom, the miracles he did, and his radiant countenance, I say to myself, "I'd give anything in the world for that kind of anointing." His secret, however, emerged at the end of his life. While his enemies threw stones at him, he prayed—seconds before his last breath—"Lord, do not hold this sin against them" (Acts 7:60). And therein lies the secret to his unusual anointing.

If you are still asking, "How can I know that I have totally forgiven my enemy (my betrayer, my unfaithful spouse, my unkind parent, the one who ruined my life, or the one who has hurt our children)?" I answer, "Walking out these seven principles is as near as you can come to exhibiting *total forgiveness*."

I must add one caution: never go to a person you have had to forgive and say, "I forgive you." This will be counterproductive every time unless it is to a person that you know is yearning for you to forgive him or her. Otherwise, you will create a stir with which you will not be able to cope. The person will say to you, "For what?" It is my experience that nine out of ten people I have had to forgive sincerely do not feel they have done anything wrong. It is up to me to forgive them from my heart—and then keep quiet about it.

PERSONAL REFLECTION

Fashion a prayer in your own words asking God to help you forgive and keep forgiving.

_____

_____

_____

_____

_____

_____

_____

_____

_____

_____

_____

_____

_____

_____

_____

_____

SECTION V

Are You Ready to Be Set Free From the Past?

DAY 31

Overcoming the Accuser

G OD DOES NOT want you to feel guilty. But Satan does. Making you feel guilty could almost be called his job description. His chief weapon: accusing you, making you feel guilty, telling you how bad you are, how unworthy and how stupid you are to believe God's promises. That is his job. Never forget it.

The purpose of today's entry in our journey to total forgiveness is to help you see what Satan is up to—and not let him succeed with you. I will make some general observations about the devil—what I think you need to know if you are struggling to forgive. There are two cautions before I proceed.

1. Don't think that you should become an expert on the devil. Those who have this aspiration are not, in my opinion, truly mature Christians. Indeed, people like this are often the ones who get in over their heads and are overcome, like the sons of Sceva. (See Acts 19:13–16.)

2. You do need, however, a basic knowledge of his ways. Paul could say, "We are not unaware of his schemes" (2 Cor. 2:11).

For the purpose of this book here is how I would describe his ways.

1. He would prefer that you believe he does not exist. Unbelief in the devil is the devil's work. If you don't believe in the reality of Satan, you have just told me he has succeeded with you.

2. If you do believe he exists, then he wants to dominate your thinking; he will want you to think about him all the time—and to make you afraid of him. Always bluffing, he will intimidate you and make you think he is all-powerful. He is not; when compared with almighty God, he is a weakling but is still given limited authority on this planet for a limited time. Some people in their fear of the devil's power give the impression that they ascribe more credit to Satan than to God.

3. He is always under God's sovereign thumb; he can proceed no further than what God allows (Job 1–2). Therefore, know that the buck stops with God. Whatever trial you are going through, never forget that God gave Satan permission before He let him have a go at you. God knows you are big enough for it, or He would not have let it happen (1 Cor. 10:13).

4. Satan is a liar (John 8:44). Sometimes, however, he will quote Scripture (Matt. 4:6). Some of his accusations concerning you will be true. He will bring up your past. It is essential to remember about Satan that all he does is to work against the interests of Jesus Christ, his archenemy, who

is the embodiment of truth as much as Satan is the embodiment of lies.

5. His main tactic insofar as the Christian is concerned is to accuse. His manner is the quintessential example of pointing the finger. He keeps a record of wrongs, has a memory better than yours, and will remind you of things you thought you had forgotten. He has one goal: to bring you down and keep you from pure joy. Remember, he does not want you to forgive yourself.

6. He is resistible. He will come to you like a roaring lion (1 Pet. 5:8), making you think you are defeated before you have had a chance to count to ten. This is an example of how he will lie to you. But you are to resist him. He will make you think he is irresistible—that is a lie. Resist him, and you will find out. The proof he is a weakling is that he has to flee once he sees you are on to him.

7. Spiritual warfare is essentially defensive. This means that you must not go on the attack. Attacking him is foolish. I know too many stories of people who were going to have a go at Satan and today have lost their ministries because they promoted themselves above the level of their competence—attacking Satan. You have no promise that he will flee when you attack him, only when he attacks you. This is so important that I will remind you of this in a few days.

One of the more disquieting aspects of modern Christianity in some places is the high profile given to the devil and "spiritual warfare." One gets the impression sometimes that all things that go against our will are of the devil. He gets more attention than God sometimes! Most of all, I wonder if some people fear the devil more than they do God.

I would not want you to be unaware of the devil's power, however. My dad used to say to me that the devil is "very crafty, second only to God in power and wisdom." Yes. Quite. But don't forget he is *second* to God—a far second and nowhere equal to Him (1 John 4:4). It is God to whom he answers, and it is God to whom we answer.

Satan is called the "accuser of our brothers" in Revelation 12:10. This phrase has been immense comfort to the people of God over the centuries. Anybody who has had any experience in the wiles of the devil can tell you this is his chief tactic—to accuse. But there are two ways to defeat him: through the blood of Jesus and the testimony of the people of God. In other words, not only was it the blood of Jesus that defeated Satan, but it was also faith in Jesus' blood.

When Satan accuses you, remind him that your sins have been forgiven by God—through the shed blood of Jesus. Don't point him to your good works, your best efforts, your resolve to do better, or the fact that you have improved over the years. Point him to the blood of Jesus. Nothing more. Rest your case there. You know that you are a great sinner, but you have a great God and a great Savior, and all your sins are washed away.

PERSONAL REFLECTION

We all have thoughts and feelings about our identity and self-image. After reading today's message, do you now recognize some things you have believed about yourself as lies from the accuser? Make a list of these lies. When the enemy reminds you of them, tell him (and yourself) that you are forgiven by God and your past does not define who you are.

_____

_____

_____

_____

_____

_____

_____

_____

_____

_____

_____

_____

_____

_____

The First R of Spiritual Warfare: Recognize

YESTERDAY WE DISCUSSED our accuser, the devil, and his ways. The apostle Paul made an interesting comment in this matter: "We are not unaware of his schemes" (2 Cor. 2:11). It is a sign of considerable maturity to be able to recognize the devil, refuse to listen to him, and resist him. These are what I call the three Rs of spiritual warfare: recognize, refuse, and resist. I am indebted to Dr. Harry Kilbride for sharing these lovely insights in a sermon I heard him preach many years ago. I have never forgotten it. I will expand on the three Rs over the next three days. Today we'll look at the first R: recognize.

This means to recognize whether the devil is behind the thoughts you are having. It is not always easy to know that it is the devil when you have a particular thought. You might think it is God or that it is your own thought. And indeed it very well may be. It is very possible to have your own thoughts that come from inside you—quite apart from God or the devil. So be aware of this. But know also that the devil can exploit your weaknesses and put thoughts in your head in an effort to mislead you.

The devil speaks to you in basically two ways: through putting thoughts in your head when you are alone and through another person's comments. So how do you recognize that it is Satan and not God who is giving you certain thoughts? Here is how to know it is the devil and not God.

1. When you feel "put down" or demoralized. God would never do that. Jesus never did that. Whenever you feel hurt or less than respected by a word or thought that comes into your head, it is the devil.

2. When you feel oppressed. I remind you of what Dr. Martyn Lloyd-Jones used to teach me: "God never oppresses us." This was so emancipating for me. When a spirit of heaviness hovers over you, mark it down: it is not God doing this—it is the devil.

3. When you feel criticized. This is the accuser at work. When you feel criticized, you are sad, hurt, and singled out as unclean—that is the devil. When God speaks to you, it will be a feeling of being affirmed and of hope, and He will show you a way forward.

4. When there is no positive way forward. Let us say that you are given a word or thought that not only is unhelpful but also leaves you without any remedy. When there is no remedy provided in the word that comes to you, this I can only call "vintage Satan." He never shows a way forward; he only wants to keep you feeling that there is nothing you can do. That is one of the things he does best.

5. When the thought that comes to you puts you in bondage. Satan loves to keep us bound—unable to move freely. (See Luke 13:16.) He does that with our spirit, giving us an inner feeling of bondage and immobility. When you cannot forgive yourself, you are sometimes almost immobile—at least internally. You are unmotivated and unable to get things done. You are devoid of expectancy and aspiration. That is exactly where Satan wants you.

On the other hand, when God comes, there will be joy and liberty (2 Cor. 3:17). This is as opposite to the devil's work as you can get. You will never be demoralized by the Holy Spirit—even when He shows you your sin. This is because the way He does it gives us hope; He convicts us, shows us the way forward, points us to the blood of Jesus, lets us save face, and sets us free.

PERSONAL REFLECTION

Has today's message opened your eyes to the spiritual warfare going on behind your struggle to forgive? Describe in your own words the difference between the conviction of the Holy Spirit and the condemnation of the enemy.

_____

_____

_____

The Second R of Spiritual Warfare: Refuse

REFUSE IS THE second R of spiritual warfare. It simply means that you refuse to dwell on the thought the devil puts in your head. The moment you have concluded, "This is the devil, not God," your next move is to refuse to give any time to the thought.

The devil wants to see how bothered you are by the accusation. When he throws a fiery dart (Eph. 6:16) at you, he wants it to "stick" so that you feel the pain of it for a long time. It is better, of course, to see the attack coming so you can put the shield of faith up in advance. But this is not always possible. He often manages to get a cutting word to us—and we feel the pain. But the pain will go away when you refuse to dwell on it.

I was once given a broadside attack in a book review. What was said was not even true. But it hurt. I had two choices: to dwell on it and start feeling sorry for myself that people would believe it, or to refuse to dwell on what the writer said. I chose the latter. I promise you, it stopped hurting at once! And when I do think of it, which I do once in a while, I let myself have a good laugh. The devil doesn't want that!

Sometimes, however, Satan ruthlessly attacks us in the middle of the night, either through dreams or thoughts that keep us awake. This is hard. I struggle here. When I am tired and vulnerable in the middle of the night, it is often difficult to think clearly and act in the manner that I know is right. Satan never plays fair! All one can do is plead for the mercy of God, who enables us to find grace in the time of need (Heb. 4:16).

I was privileged to meet Oral Roberts years ago. He invited Louise and me into his home. I wanted to thank him for his endorsement of my book *Total Forgiveness*. We got to talking about sleep and getting enough sleep. He counseled me to do what I have heard before, but it was so timely: start quoting Scripture! When you do that, the devil flees—and you go back to sleep.

The point is once you recognize the devil as being the culprit for your being "down" or "low," refuse him with all your might. Get out an old hymnal and read through the hymns—or sing them! Or turn to a good book. Mrs. Martyn Lloyd-Jones once shared a problem she used to have and how Satan would bring this fear before her. She told me she learned to "refuse to think about it." "Just start thinking about anything else," she would say to me. "Anything else."

When an evil thought disturbs you, you must turn the devil off—like pushing the delete button on a computer. Absolutely refuse to entertain or dwell on an evil thought. This would be true whether it is holding a grudge, dwelling on what someone has done to you, concentrating on the negative, feeling sorry for yourself, or blaming God for everything unpleasant that has happened to you.

PERSONAL REFLECTION

Write a declaration-style prayer based on scriptures about your mind, such as 1 Corinthians 2:16 and Philippians 4:8. For example: "I have the mind of Christ, and with God's help, I will only think about things that are true, noble, right, pure, lovely, admirable, excellent, or praiseworthy."

_____

_____

_____

_____

_____

_____

_____

_____

_____

_____

_____

_____

The Third R of Spiritual Warfare: Resist

RESIST IS THE third R of spiritual warfare. All spiritual warfare is *defensive*. This is extremely important. You are never called to go on the offensive in combating Satan, unless it means that you march into his territory to preach the gospel. That is different. We are all called to go into the world to preach the gospel (Mark 16:15). Furthermore, any obedience to God will offend the devil.

However, I lovingly warn you: if you attack Satan, like some who want to have a go at the devil, you are in a perilous situation. I repeat, you have no promise that he will flee when you go on the attack, but you have a wonderful promise that he will flee when he attacks you. The term *resist* is found in two places in the New Testament.

> Resist the devil, and he will flee from you.
> —JAMES 4:7

> Your enemy the devil prowls around like a roaring lion looking for someone to devour. Resist him, standing firm in the faith.
> —1 PETER 5:8–9

You will note the word *standing* in 1 Peter 5:9. This is a very important word for you to remember when it comes to resisting the devil. You are required to stand. In the most famous spiritual warfare passage in the New Testament the word *stand* is found four times.

> Put on the full armor of God, so that you can take your *stand* against the devil's schemes.... Therefore put on the full armor of God, so that when the day of evil comes, you may be able to *stand* your ground, and after you have done everything, to *stand*. *Stand* firm then.
> —EPHESIANS 6:11–14, EMPHASIS ADDED

To stand means what it says—to stand. You don't walk, you don't run, you don't crawl, you don't fall, and you don't go backward. You stand. That is all you are required to do. For standing is resisting. When you stand up against his attack, you are resisting. Your only job is to keep from moving, either by going forward, dropping behind, tripping, or falling.

To put it another way, when Satan attacks, don't try to make a lot of progress. Don't even move. Just stay put. Resisting the devil is great progress when he attacks. This is the way he overreaches himself. It is when you stand. You say, "Christ died for my sins." You may say, "Your accusations are true, but Jesus died and shed His blood for my sins."

There is one thing more you can do: forgive yourself, as we discussed on days 17–19. Make the decision to do it. It is something you must choose to do, not something you wait until you feel "led" to do. You must do it now. Forgive yourself. Wherever you are as you read today's portion of this journey—at home, on public transportation, on your lunch hour—wherever, do it now, and resist the devil. On what authority?

On the authority of God's Word. By what rationale? By the rationale that forgiving yourself is precisely the opposite of what Satan wants. Do the opposite of what you know he wants, and you will be safe and secure in God's everlasting arms.

As I mentioned earlier, you'll need to keep forgiving yourself and others for life. Whenever the devil reminds you of what you or someone else has done, and it brings you down, you need to forgive all over again. You may go for a good while not feeling any hurt or shame from the past, but should the devil bring something to your attention with the express purpose of causing you to lose your joy and freedom, simply forgive all over again. That is what we all have to do.

One last thing: The devil knows his time is short (Rev. 12:12). He knows his final destiny (Matt. 8:29; Rev. 20:10). The next time the devil reminds you of your past, remind him of his future.

Remember the three Rs of spiritual warfare. The devil *is* resistible. "Resist the devil, and he will flee from you" (Jas. 4:7). It is true! But it begins with recognizing him and then refusing to listen to him.

PERSONAL REFLECTION

Which of your past mistakes has been the hardest for you to forgive yourself for? Have you had to forgive yourself more than once for it?

_____

_____

_____

_____

_____

_____

_____

_____

_____

How will you stand against these accusations of the enemy in the future?

_____

_____

_____

_____

_____

_____

_____

_____

Ten Steps to Freedom

THE TEACHING AND carrying out of forgiveness has been recognized as valid and therapeutic even outside the realm of the Christian faith. In my book *Total Forgiveness*, I write about a *Daily Express* article about a course in Leeds.[1] The reason for this course, which was paid for by a grant from the John Templeton Foundation, was apparently the belief that forgiveness can be good for your health. Holding a grudge, it is said, leads to illnesses ranging from common colds to heart disease because of all the stored-up anger and stress. Dr. Sandi Mann, a psychologist at the University of Central Lancashire, believes that there is a strong link between our emotions and our immune system. All of this goes to show the benefits of forgiving people—even if we were not motivated by Jesus and the New Testament!

Here are ten steps to freedom, as found in the *Daily Express* article:

1. Stop excusing, pardoning, or rationalizing.
2. Pinpoint the actions that have hurt you.
3. Spend time thinking of ways in which your life would be more satisfying if you could let go of your grievances.

4. Try replacing angry thoughts about the "badness" of the perpetrator with thoughts about how the offender is also a human being who is vulnerable to harm.

5. Identify with the offender's probable state of mind. Understand the perpetrator's history while not condoning his or her actions.

6. Spend some time developing greater compassion toward the perpetrator.

7. Become more aware that you have needed other people's forgiveness in the past.

8. Make a heartfelt resolution not to pass on your own pain.

9. Spend time appreciating the sense of purpose and direction that comes after steps 1–8.

10. Enjoy the sense of emotional relief that comes when the burden of a grudge has melted away. Enjoy also the feeling of goodwill and mercy you have shown.

There is a wonderful phrase in the Book of Hebrews, "How much more" (Heb. 9:14; 10:29). The point the writer is making is that if certain things were true under the Mosaic Law, how much more is promised now that Christ has come and fulfilled it?

It seems to me that if the secular world is catching on to the teachings of Jesus—even if they are not acknowledging Him or the Holy Spirit—and deriving benefits from that teaching, *how much more* should Christians experience this? If non-Christians can find peace because it is better for their health, *how much more* should you and I—who want to please

God and honor the Holy Spirit—embrace this teaching with all our hearts? It surely leaves us all without excuse.

The most profound thing I ever heard Joni Eareckson Tada say is this: "I am a Christian not because of what it does for me but because it is true." We should believe Christ's teaching because it is true.

PERSONAL REFLECTION

Imagine you are giving advice to someone younger than you. What advice would you give him or her about forgiveness?

_____

_____

_____

_____

What specific steps have you taken to totally forgive? What steps will you continue to take?

_____

_____

_____

_____

DAY 36

Principles of Total Forgiveness

L ET'S LOOK AT six key principles of total forgiveness.

1. Make the deliberate and irrevocable choice not to tell anyone what they did.

Anyone who truly forgives does not gossip about his or her offenders. Talking about how you have been wounded with the purpose of hurting your enemies' reputation or credibility is just a form of punishing them. Most of us do not talk about what happened for therapeutic reasons, but rather to keep our enemies from being admired. We divulge what they did so others will think less of them. That is an attempt to punish—which is usurping God's arena of action.

Refusing to punish those who deserve it—giving up the natural desire to see them "get what's coming to them"—is the essence of total forgiveness. Our human nature cannot bear the thought that people who hurt us deeply would get away with what they have done. It seems so unfair! We want vengeance—namely, their just punishment. But the fear that they won't get punished is the opposite of perfect love. This is why John said:

163

> There is no fear in love. But perfect love drives out
> fear, because fear has to do with *punishment*. The
> one who fears is not made perfect in love.
> —1 John 4:18, emphasis added

If you harbor the desire to see your enemies punished, you will eventually lose the anointing of the Spirit. But when perfect love—the love of Jesus and the fruit of the Holy Spirit—enters, the desire for your enemy to be punished leaves. Total forgiveness is refusing to punish. It is refusing to cave in to the fear that this person or those people won't get their comeuppance—the punishment or rebuke you think they deserve.

I have been intrigued by John's assertion that fear "has to do with punishment." Sometimes we fear that God won't step in and give our enemies their just deserts. But if one gives in to this fear, he will be trespassing on God's territory, and God doesn't like that. Vindication is God's prerogative and God's prerogative alone. Deuteronomy 32:35 tells us, "It is mine to avenge; I will repay." This verse is even cited twice in the New Testament (Rom. 12:19; Heb. 10:30). Vindication is what God does best. He doesn't want our help.

So when you refuse to be instruments of punishment, God likes that; it sets Him free to decide what should be done. But if you maneuver your way into the process, He may well let you do what you will; then neither divine vengeance nor true justice will be carried out—only the fulfillment of your personal grudge.

It is important that you examine yourself in this area. You must ask, "How much of what I am about to say or do is just an attempt to punish?" If punishment is your motive, you are about to grieve the Holy Spirit, however much right may be on your side.

2. Be pleasant to them should you be around them.

Do not say or do anything that would make them anxious. Put them at their ease. This can be hard to do, certainly harder than the first step. It is we who are afraid when we can't forgive. When we pass our fear to them, it is utterly the opposite of what Jesus would do. He would say, "Fear not." God does not want us to fear; we must not do or say anything to cause others to fear. Be nice. Put them at ease. This is what Jesus did when He turned up after His resurrection to ten disciples behind closed doors. (See John 20:19.)

3. If conversation ensues, say that which would set them free from guilt.

Guilt is most painful, and we can easily punish people by sending them on a guilt trip. Never do that. Remember that Jesus doesn't want us to feel guilty. When we are going to be Jesus to others, then we will not want them to be angry with themselves.

This is a hard one. We get some satisfaction when we think they feel really, really bad. That defuses us and eases our anger somewhat. But if we want to be valiant and utterly magnanimous—thus showing true godliness—we will say whatever is the equivalent of Joseph's words: "Do not be angry with yourselves" (Gen. 45:5). Joseph would not allow his brothers to feel guilty, and this is a choice we too must make. It's hard, but it is what we would want if things were reversed and we needed forgiveness. "Do to others as you would have them do to you" (Luke 6:31).

4. Let them feel good about themselves.

Not only does this mean *never* reminding them of their wrong and your hurt, but it also means helping them through any guilt they may have. This can be done without any reference to what they did. If it is not in the open, as with Joseph's situation, that is of course different; he let his brothers save face by showing God's sovereign strategy in their sin. But in many cases you will not be able to talk about anything specifically. You can still let them save face because you know that they know what they did.

You therefore must behave as though you don't even think they did anything wrong! That is hard for all of us, but it must be done. Say whatever you can (as long as it is true) that will give that person a sense of dignity. That is the point of Galatians 6:1: "Brothers and sisters, if someone is caught in a sin, you who live by the Spirit should restore that person gently. But watch yourselves, or you also may be tempted." As long as there is a trace of self-righteousness and pointing the finger, your attempt at total forgiveness will backfire.

5. Protect them from their greatest fear.

This is what total forgiveness is all about: setting people free. If you are aware of some deep, dark secret and fear they have, they will probably know that you know. If they can tell by your graciousness that their secret will never be revealed— ever—to anyone, they will be relieved. You only tell them when you know they know what you know, and you are convinced this would make them feel better. If by reminding them, it would obviously not make them feel better, don't even come close!

Remember that Joseph knew his brothers' greatest fear was that their father, Jacob, would learn the truth of their evil deed. Joseph never mentioned this directly but suggested they speak to Jacob in such a way that they wouldn't have to tell him after all. (See Genesis 45:9–13.) It must have given the brothers incalculable relief to know that they were not obliged to tell Jacob.

6. Keep it up today, tomorrow, this year, and next year.

As we have said, total forgiveness is a lifelong commitment. Some days will be easier than others. There will come a time when you think you are completely over it and have won a total victory—only to find the very next day Satan reminds you of what they did and the utter injustice that they will be unpunished and never exposed. The temptation to bitterness will emerge. After all, we're not perfect! If we say we have no sin—that we are incapable of the same old bitterness—we are deceived (1 John 1:8).

This is exactly why I read Luke 6:37 every day: "Do not judge, and you will not be judged. Do not condemn, and you will not be condemned. Forgive, and you will be forgiven." All commitments to forgive need renewal. In my case daily. I am not telling you that this is what *you* must do, but be warned: the devil is cunning. He will come through the back door unexpectedly and try to upset you for forgiving. When you forgave your enemy, you then and there removed that open invitation to the devil to get inside. Satan's favorite rationale is bitterness—he therefore will keep trying to get back into your thought life.

Whether it be Luke 6:37 or another way forward, in your case—even if you aren't required to keep it up each day—I can tell you right now that it is only a matter of time before your commitment to forgive will need to be renewed.

PERSONAL REFLECTION

Pause and evaluate your progress in these areas of forgiveness. How are you doing? Write down the ways you have improved as well as the areas where you know you still need to grow.

The Ultimate Proof

"BUT I TELL you, love your enemies and pray for those who persecute you" (Matt. 5:44). When you do this from the heart—praying for their being blessed and off the hook—you're there. It is not a perfunctory prayer, not a "We commit them to You" prayer, and certainly not an "Oh God, please deal with them" prayer. It is praying that God will forgive them—that is, *overlook* what they have done and bless and prosper them as though they'd never sinned at all.

Praying for the ones who have hurt you or let you down is the greatest challenge of all, for three reasons:

- You take a route utterly against the flesh.

- Nobody will ever know you are doing it.

- Your heart could break when God answers that prayer and truly blesses them as if they'd never sinned.

And yet Jesus' word to pray for such people is not a polite suggestion; it is a command—and one that may seem so outrageous that you want to dismiss it out of hand. Some see it as a lofty, but unrealistic, goal.

I remember a church leader turning to me to pray about his son-in-law who had been unfaithful to his daughter. He said to me that his own prayer was only that God would "deal" with this man. "This is where I have come to," he said to me, "that God will deal with him."

I understood what he meant, and I felt for him. I find what people do to our own offspring the hardest things to forgive. I therefore understood what he was feeling. A few days later it was reported that this leader's son-in-law had been in a serious accident. This same church leader was on the phone, glad that the accident had happened. Now, in this particular case there was nothing sinister in this euphoria. He simply hoped that the accident would wake up his son-in-law to put his marriage back together. It was so understandable.

But this is not what Jesus means. He is commanding us to pray that our enemy will be *blessed*. If, however, you should pray that he or she will be cursed or punished instead of blessed, just remember that is how your enemy possibly feels about you. After all, have *you* ever been someone's enemy? Have *you* ever done something that brought a fellow Christian to tears and brokenness? If so, how would you like that person to pray for *you*? That God will deal with *you*? That God will cause *you* to have an accident? Yet how would it make you feel if the person prayed that you would be blessed and let off the hook? That you would prosper as if you'd never sinned? Would you not like that? "Do to others as you would have them do to you" (Luke 6:31).

Jesus wants a sincere prayer from us. It is like signing your name to a document, having it witnessed, and never looking back. You are not allowed to tell the world, "Guess what I did? I have actually prayed for my unfaithful spouse to be blessed." No. It is quiet. Only the angels witness it, but it makes God very happy.

After all, every parent wants his or her children to get along with one another. No parent likes it when one child comes and squeals on the other and demands that he or she be punished. The poor parent is put on the spot. What gladdens the heart of every parent is when there is love and forgiveness and the parent is not put on the spot to have to take sides and punish anyone. That is what we do for God when we ask that He bless and not curse. He told us to pray for our enemies, "that you may be children of your Father in heaven. He causes his sun to rise on the evil and the good, and sends rain on the righteous and the unrighteousness" (Matt. 5:45).

PERSONAL REFLECTION

Have you come to the place where you can pray for those who have hurt you most deeply? List the names of people for whom you have the hardest time praying.

_____

_____

_____

_____

_____

Five Stages of Praying for Your Enemies

THERE ARE FIVE stages, or levels, of praying for one's enemies:

1. Duty—The first level is strictly based on obedience; you are doing it because you feel you have to.

2. Debt—You have reached the second level when you are so conscious of what you have been forgiven of that you cannot help but pray for your enemy. You don't want God to "spill the beans" on you, so you pray that your enemy too will be spared.

3. Desire—You begin to pray for your enemy because it is what you really want.

4. Delight—This takes desire a step further. It is when you love doing it! You get joy from praying for and blessing your enemy.

5. Durability—This means that what you took on as a lifelong commitment becomes a lifestyle. The thought of turning back or praying in a different way is out of the question. It has become

a habit, and it no longer seems like something extraordinary. What began as a duty and once seemed insurmountable is now almost second nature.

All this is done in secret, behind the scenes. Only the angels know. It is quiet intercession. You aren't allowed to get your reward or applause from people who may think, "Oh, isn't that lovely you would pray for your enemy like that!" No. It is a secret that must never be told. Enter your place of prayer, and shut the door behind you. "Then your Father, who sees what is done in secret, will reward you" (Matt. 6:4).

There are several consequences of praying for your enemies or people who have disappointed you. The most obvious consequence is your reward in heaven. But another consequence is that—be warned—God may answer your prayer! "Oh no!" you may say. "I only prayed for them because I was being obedient. Surely God would not actually bless and prosper that wicked person." Well, He may indeed! The question is, Will you still pray the prayer?

Let's turn the tables around and assume you have hurt somebody. If the person prayed for your prosperity, you wouldn't object, would you? How do you know this hasn't already happened? How do you know that the blessing and fulfillment you are experiencing are not the answer to prayer on your behalf by someone who has been hurt by you? You may say, "They would never pray for me like that." Perhaps. But the very fact that you are blessed and yet have caused hurt in someone else's life is proof that God hasn't chosen to throw the book at you yet. Be thankful for that, and pray for your enemies in return.

Another surprising consequence of your prayer is that—just

maybe—your enemy may become your friend. That is what God did to us.

> God was reconciling the world to himself in Christ, not counting people's sins against them. And he has committed to us the message of reconciliation.
> —2 Corinthians 5:19

You too may well win your enemy over by loving and praying for him or her. "I don't want this person as a friend," you may say now. That's OK. We saw earlier that total forgiveness does not always mean reconciliation. Do not feel guilty if you don't want to become close friends. But in some cases this has happened. And if there is a reconciliation or a friendship that eventually results, that person may say to you, "You were brilliant the whole time. You were loving and caring, never vindictive." One rule of thumb to follow: treat your enemy now the way you will be glad you did should you become good friends.

The greatest positive consequence is the knowledge that you have pleased God. I want to be like Enoch, who was "commended as one who pleased God" (Heb. 11:5). Nothing pleases God more than our loving and praying for our enemies. It is significant that Job's troubles stopped when he prayed for his friends who were persecutors and tormentors during his suffering. "After Job had prayed for his friends, the Lord restored his fortunes and gave him twice as much as he had before" (Job 42:10).

Doing this is, of course, our duty—but it eventually becomes a delight. If you hate, you will give your enemy your heart and mind. As Nelson Mandela said, don't give those two things away.[1]

Forgiveness is not *total* forgiveness until we bless our

enemies—and pray for them to be blessed. Forgiving them is a major step; *totally* forgiving them has been fully achieved when we set God free to bless them. But in this we are the first to be blessed and those who totally forgive are blessed the most.

PERSONAL REFLECTION

In practical terms how do you intend to get better at praying for enemies until it becomes a lifelong delight?

_____

_____

_____

_____

_____

_____

_____

_____

_____

_____

DAY 39

Love Says, "Let It Go!"

FIRST CORINTHIANS 13, the great love chapter of the Bible, is a perfect demonstration of the cause and effect of total forgiveness. The apex of this wonderful passage is the phrase found in verse 5: love "keeps no record of wrongs." The Greek word that is translated as "record" is *logizomai*, which means to reckon or impute. This word is important to Paul's doctrine of justification by faith. For the person who believes, his or her faith is "credited" to him or her as righteousness (Rom. 4:5).

This is the same word used in 1 Corinthians 13:5. It is turned around in Romans 4:8, again using the same word: "Blessed is the one whose sin the Lord will never count against him." Therefore, *not* to reckon, impute, or "count" the wrongs of a loved one is to do for that person what God does for us—namely, choose not to recognize the sin. In God's sight our sin no longer exists. When we totally forgive someone, we too refuse to keep a record of the person's wrongs.

It must be clearly acknowledged that wrong was done, that evil took place. Total forgiveness obviously sees the evil but chooses to erase it. Before a grudge becomes lodged in the heart, the offense must be willfully forgotten. Resentment must not be given an opportunity to set in. The love described in 1 Corinthians 13 can only come by following a lifestyle of total forgiveness.

Why keep records, even mental ones, when others wrong you? To use them later. "I'll remember that," you say—and you are true to your word. And it usually comes up sooner rather than later. You may not ever consciously think it, but you essentially say in your heart, "God isn't doing His job," and you help God out by punishing that person who hurt you—whether it be a spouse, a relative, a church leader, a former schoolteacher, or an insensitive boss.

Love is a choice. It is an act of the will. Keeping a record of wrongs is also an act of the will—a choice *not* to love— and it is the more natural, easy choice for you to make. But two very simple things, I believe, will help you stop keeping a record of wrongs:

1. When a person does wrong, refuse to point it out *to the person*.
2. When a person does wrong, refuse to point it out *to others*.

This even applies to imaginary conversations—those internal dialogues with yourself in which you can't get what the person did off your mind. You may fantasize what you will say or do to him or her, or what you might tell other people about the person. This conversation may go on and on—and hours and days may pass when you neither accomplish anything nor feel any better!

For those who find such conversations therapeutic, I would only remind you to let your thoughts be positive and wholesome; keep no record of wrongs in your *thoughts*, and you will be less likely to expose such records by your *words*.

When I am tempted to say something negative and I refuse to speak, I can often feel the release of the Holy Spirit within my heart. It is as if God says to me, "Well done." It is a very good feeling! After all, Jesus is touched with our weaknesses (Heb. 4:15), and He also lets us feel His joy when we overcome them! He rewards us with an incredible peace and the witness of the Spirit in our hearts.

Not keeping a record of wrongs is also a refusal to keep a record of the things you have done right. It is just as dishonoring to God's grace to keep a record of your rights as it is to keep a record of others' wrongs. Why? Because it is a form of self-exaltation. You are implicitly saying, "I told you so," in order to make someone else look bad. It takes spiritual maturity to refrain from saying, "I told you so."

More than a few people not only keep a record of wrongs but also have an even longer list of times when they have been right! We all want other people to know how right we have been. We want them to know that we said it first. It is amazing to me the advice that comes after the fact: "I knew it all along." "Do you see now how right I was?" "You should have listened to me." "I told you so!"

Love tears up not only the record of wrongs but also the list of rights. True forgivers destroy the record they might have used to vindicate themselves. If there is no record of rights lodged firmly in your head, you will not be able to refer to it later to prove how right you were. Forget what the person did that was wrong, and forget what you did that was right. Paul said, "I do not even judge myself" (1 Cor. 4:3). I have often concluded that very few people really deserve the vindication they think they are entitled to. I can only say that if vindication is truly deserved, then that vindication will surely come, for God is just.

Love "keeps no record of wrongs" (1 Cor. 13:5). Why do

we keep track of the times we are offended? To use them. To prove what happened. To wave them before someone who doubts what actually happened.

A husband may say to his wife in a moment of anger, "I'll remember that." And he does! She may say to him, "I will never forget this." And she doesn't!

Many marriages could be healed overnight if *both* parties would stop pointing the finger. Blaming others has been a common problem throughout human history, but God blesses the one who does away with the pointing of the finger. (See Isaiah 58:9.)

Love is a choice. Total forgiveness is a choice. It is not a feeling—at least at first—but is rather an act of the will. It is the choice to tear up the record of wrongs we have been keeping. We clearly see and acknowledge the evil that was done to us, but we erase it—or destroy the record—before it becomes lodged in our hearts. This way resentment does not have a chance to grow. When we develop a lifestyle of total forgiveness, we learn to erase the wrong rather than file it away in our mental computer. When we do this all the time—as a lifestyle—not only do we avoid bitterness, but we also eventually experience total forgiveness as a feeling—and it is a good feeling.

PERSONAL REFLECTION

Do you have a mental scorecard on which you are always the winner? Is everyone else a loser, according to your score-keeping system? What reasons have you used to allow yourself to keep a list of "rights"? What can you do now to banish those excuses and truly repent?

_____

_____

_____

_____

_____

_____

_____

_____

Read Isaiah 58:9 and pray, asking God to help you stop keeping records of wrongs and develop total forgiveness according to His Word.

_____

_____

_____

_____

_____

_____

_____

_____

_____

_____

Have you ever had imaginary conversations that were eventually realized? What was the outcome? What does that tell you about the power of your thought life? Read Romans 12:2 and think about how it relates to these kinds of internal dialogues—even if they are never spoken out loud. Pray for God's help to control your tongue and your thought life, and ask Him to reveal the ways they have been blocking your ability to forgive others.

_____

_____

_____

_____

_____

_____

_____

_____

Day 40

Let the Past Be the Past—at Last

Total forgiveness must take place in the heart or it is worthless, for "out of the overflow of the heart the mouth speaks" (Matt. 12:34, BSB). If we have not truly forgiven those who hurt us in our hearts, it will come out—sooner or later. But if it has indeed taken place in the heart, our words will show it. When there is bitterness, it will eventually manifest itself; when there is love, "there is nothing in them to make them stumble" (1 John 2:10).

This is why reconciliation is not essential for total forgiveness. If forgiveness truly takes place in the heart, one does not need to know whether one's enemy will reconcile. If I have forgiven him in my heart of hearts, but he still doesn't want to speak to me, I can still have the inner victory. It may be far easier to forgive when we know that those who maligned or betrayed us are sorry for what they did, but if I must have this knowledge before I can forgive, I may never have the victory over my bitterness.

Those who believe that they are not required to forgive unless their offenders have first repented are not following Jesus' example on the cross.

> Jesus said, "Father, forgive them, for they do not know what they are doing." And they divided up his clothes by casting lots.
>
> —Luke 23:34

If Jesus had waited until His enemies felt some guilt or shame for their words and actions, He never would have forgiven them.

It is my experience that most people we must forgive do not believe they have done anything wrong at all, or if they know that they did something wrong, they believe it was justified. I would even go so far as to say that at least 90 percent of all the people I've ever had to forgive would be indignant at the thought that they had done something wrong. If you gave them a lie detector test, they would honestly say that they had done nothing wrong—and they would pass the test with flying colors.

Total forgiveness, therefore, must take place in the heart. If I have a genuine heart experience, I will not be devastated if there is no reconciliation. If those who hurt me don't want to continue a relationship with me, it isn't my problem because I have forgiven them. This is also why a person can achieve inner peace even when forgiving someone who has died. The apostle John wrote, "Dear friends, if our *hearts* do not condemn us, we have confidence before God" (1 John 3:21, emphasis added). Confidence toward God is ultimately what total forgiveness is all about; He is the One I want to please at the end of the day. He cares and knows whether I have truly and totally forgiven, and when I *know* I have His love and approval, I am one very happy and contented servant of Christ.

The sweet consequence of not keeping a record of all wrongs is that we let go of the past and its effect on the present. We cast our care on God and rely on Him to restore the wasted years and to cause everything to turn out for good. We find ourselves, almost miraculously, accepting ourselves as we are (just as God does), with all our failures (just as God does), knowing all the while our potential to make more mistakes. God never becomes disillusioned with us; He loves us and knows us inside out.

Moses had a past. He was a murderer. (See Exodus 2:11–12.) But years later he would proclaim the eighth commandment: "You shall not murder" (Exod. 20:13). David had a past, but he also had a future after his shame: "Then I will teach transgressors your ways, so that sinners will turn back to you," he wrote (Ps. 51:13). Jonah deliberately ran from God, but he was still used in an astonishing revival (Jon. 3). Peter's disgrace—denying Jesus—did not abort God's plans for him. But all these men had to forgive themselves before they could move into the ministry God had planned for them.

Can you do that? Having forgiven others, it is time to forgive yourself. That is exactly what God wants of you and me. It is long overdue; let the past be the past—at last.

PERSONAL REFLECTION

As we reach the close of our journey, are there any unresolved issues of forgiveness you still need to address? Explain.

_____

_____

_____

_____

_____

_____

_____

_____

_____

_____

_____

Write a prayer summing up your specific requests for help in this area. Ask God to honor your desire to totally forgive.

_____

_____

_____

_____

_____

_____

_____

_____

_____

Notes

Introduction
What Is Total Forgiveness?

1. Corrie ten Boom, *The Hiding Place* (Boston: G. K. Hall, 1973).

2. Gary Thomas, "The Forgiveness Factor," *Christianity Today* 44, no. 1 (January 10, 2000): 38.

Day 1
Forgiveness Is *Not* Approving or Justifying What Happened

1. *Oxford English Dictionary*, s.v. "justify," accessed February 6, 2019, https://en.oxforddictionaries.com/definition/justify.

Day 2
Forgiveness Is *Not* Excusing or Pardoning What Happened

1. Clyde M. Narramore, *Every Person Is Worth Understanding* (Bloomington, IN: CrossBooks, 2011).

Day 5
Forgiveness Is *Not* Blindness to What Happened

1. Blue Letter Bible, s.v. "*kakos*," accessed January 27, 2019, https://www.blueletterbible.org/lang/lexicon/lexicon.cfm?Strongs=G2556&t=NIV.

Day 10
Stop Playing God

1. Blue Letter Bible, s.v. "*krinō*," accessed January 27, 2019, https://www.blueletterbible.org/lang/lexicon/lexicon.cfm?t=kjv&strongs=g2919.

Day 15
Beyond Forgiveness: *Loving* Your Enemies

1. Hillary Rodham Clinton, *Living History* (New York: Scribner, 2003), 236, https://books.google.com/books?id=H78s9ZbLXCIC&q.

2. Nelson Mandela, *Long Walk to Freedom: The Autobiography of Nelson Mandela* (New York: Little, Brown and Company, 2008), foreword, https://books.google.com/books?id=RHwLqVrnXgIC&pg.

Day 30
You've Forgiven When You Can
Pray for Them to Be Blessed

1. St. John Chrysostom, *The Homilies on the Gospel of St. Matthew*, vol. 1, trans. Sir George Prevost (North Charleston, SC: Createspace, 2017), 199.

Day 35
Ten Steps to Freedom

1. Susan Pape, "Can You Learn to Forgive?" *Daily Express*, June 5, 2000.

Day 38
Five Stages of Praying for Your Enemies

1. Mandela, *Long Walk to Freedom*.